GOD AND SPIRITUALITY

Srivathsav Gadiraju

Become Shakespeare .com

First published in 2021 by
BecomeShakespeare.com

One Point Six Technologies Pvt. Ltd.
Office No. 119-123, 1st Floor,
Building J2, B - Wing,
WadalaTruck Terminal, Wadala East, Mumbai,
Maharashtra, India, 400022.
T: +91 8080226699

ISBN - 978-81-94804-18-5

I dedicate this book to my grand father "Gurrala ramanaiah" garu .

Being a writer himself , he have written so many poems , articles and books in our native language …

& he is my inspiration to write books …

Thathayya ,

you have created a support system to the people around you and given a path

thank you so much for being a root to the family tree , piller to our family members and a guiding light to me …

I dedicate this book to you ...

Preface

A small VIRUS changed the way we think ,

changed the way we live

changed the way we look at things … is n't it !

COVID-19 made it clear , that our life is so fragile like a glass

So fragile that it will break in to number of pieces

& Yet so strong to keep the broken pieces together …

But above all it edified about one thing , our mortality …

Spirituality is all about that , making us understand the mortal nature of our life and taking us beyond our bodily needs and compulsions …

closer to our ultimate goal .

I am sure that , this book will assist you to know about deeper dimensions of spirituality and spiritual gurus of India and which inturn helps you to open the doors to spiritual abundance …

Before going in to the further details of this book …

I want to thank you guys for choosing this book …

Thank you so much …

About the Me

I am a network engineer by profession ,

and Author by passion ... I have written over 5 books till now ...

Apart from writing I am a youtuber , social media influencer , Fitness expert and many more ...

- Currently working in a multi national company in Bangalore , India

- Couple of years back I came across few incidents in my life :

It took a toll on me when i realized that lot of people are not interested in enhancing their lives - rather they are interested in materialistic lifestyle ...

How It all started :

- Being a health conscious person and having a knowledge of fitness over more than 12 years , i always get lot of questions to share some tips that I follow for **Fitness** ...

- Being a multi tasker , I realized that one thing at a time works best so i followed **Minfulness**

- and From my own experiences in life , I became interested in spirituality ...

I wanted to make it easy for common people to grow physically mentally and **spiritually**

I always wanted to create a public platform to promote physical health , mental health and Spiritual wisdom

and that's how I created the page , the community "BODY MIND and GOD" on facebook ...

Prologue

Hi friends ,

The fact that you are reading this means you are already in search for spiritual path and I wanted to tell you guys that you have taken one gaint step closer to spirituality .

It all started in the year 2000 , I was in early days of my schooling, when my grand mother asked me to write names of a deity in 3 books for thousand times to get spiritual abundance ... It might sound weird to you , but something magical happened that day after I have completed writings , being a innocent kid with nothing but a pure heart – I have written down the deity's name several times and with utmost devotion , I experienced something beyond words , difficult for a logical mind to understand ... I have wished for few things and they came in to reality the very next minute ... that was the first time I thought there is a big man sitting over there in sky somewhere

(Being a kid , by the way)

- But I understood the purpose of life in the year 2005 , when I came across one of the disciples of mahavatar babaji lineage , which you will get to know soon in this book ...

About the Me

GOD 9

Enlightenment 17

Chakras and Kundalini Yoga 21

Spiritual gurus and enlightened people : 27

1 . Sadhguru jaggi vasudev :

2. Ramakrishna Paramahamsa

3. Swami vivekananda

4. Mahavatar Babaji

5. Lahiri mahasaya

6 . Sri yukteswar giri

7. Paramahamsa yogananda

8. Master CVV

9 . Master EK

Epilogue 110

References : 113

1 GOD

Most of the people are just thinking that they know GOD. But in reality they have never experienced anything beyond their body and logical mind can perceive . Then how can one pray to him. If you don't know whether he is real or not .

Lot of so called spiritual people go to God with folded hands and they pray and do you know what they will ask.

They will ask for the comforts, happy life and successful relationships.

They are not spiritual nor they are religious – they are just greedy . . .
It might sound harsh . . . but it is the reality
They are not spiritual nor they are being religious . . .

Then what is spirituality . . . ? and how do we take spiritual path . . .

A very few will go a step further and starts questioning.
Who is GOD, Where is he and what is his nature ?
One should do this first.
One should do this first - If you want to follow spirituality
It is not atheism nor it is scepticism
It is called as curiosity . . . a healthy curiosity, which in turn will help you to get close with the creator himself . . .

It is called as curiosity . . . a healthy curiosity, which in turn will help you to open millions of possibilities for you

In other words you have to unlearn what you have been taught all these years about GOD and start being a seeker . . .

After that there is no need to ask him to fulfill our wishes.

Because everything that you can ask for will be at your doorstep away. The only thing that you have to do is open the Door of abundance.

All of us know that each and every individual is following his own religion and a GOD depending up on the religion that he / she is born in. Lot of people will identify themselves so much, that they will die or kill for their religion.

A few people who can see and think beyond their religion can only know what is the nature of the GOD .

We can say that religion is the level 2 and spirituality is level 1. I am not degrading any religion. I have immense respect towards my religion as well. But one can grow spiritually only if he is not confined to his religion.

Some people tell religion should not be there at all – but that is also wrong

Just think how a world without no religion looks like. Who would teach us about the creator and how can you decipher the creation.

So all the religions are being imposed on individuals right from their childhood – and that is OK

because it is how one can relate to the almighty !

But it is up to us, whether to take that knowledge that we have got from our religion and evolve in to spiritual person on our own … or follow religious path

It never really occurred to me which GOD

Let look in to the science behind prayer
What is the science behing prayer :

we are taught to pray right from the age of 9 or 10 ... for some people .

It is a known fact that, we pray to GOD not to make him happy but for own well being and happiness and if you are good enough like me : -) we also pray for the well being of our family members and friends . . .

Let's say that your prayers weren't answered in other words – all the situations in your life turned Upside down.

Will you be a devotee, then ?

In our childhood we have been told that – when ever we face a problem we can go to GOD and do prayer and offer something to him . . . to make the situation better and even to solve all the problems . . .

grant us our own pleasures and materialistic things

Who is he ?

All the holy books will tell one and the same . . . GOD is in all of us . . .

As we all know now that GOD is not some physical form that you can touch . . .

then who is he . . .

Now as we have got the doubt who is GOD

We have to start seeking instead of believing

We know that GOD is everywhere on earth and he is the one who controls the death and the birth . . .

Then why is that we are not able to see him -

Is he only confined to a physical form

If he is omnipresent why everyone is not able to feel his presence

No one really explained what is GOD, who is GOD and where is he in physical form . . .

I am not trying to degrade any religion nor I am being atheist . . .

Just like to one must go through all classes in primary education to reach the next class

We can be spiritual only if we know what is a religion. Each and every individual need to respect their religion.

Because religion is like a ladder with the help of which one can climb up in to higher dimension .

But you can only perceive what is there in that dimension when you become spiritual.

Because our logical mind will always try to find logic in everything that we see.

But spirituality is beyond logics . . .

So ?

—

GOD is not a painting that you have seen in art gallery.

Obviously GOD is will not be in a physical form to take a selfie and put it in our facebook : -)

GOD is completely a different dimension that no one can reach with human comprehension.

What is the other name that we are using to call him = " the creator " , is n't it !

" the creator "

If you look at it carefully

GOD is the creator of this planet ,

the earth that we are on - is his creation ,

the solar system that our planet is in - is his creation

galaxies, milkyway, universe . . . everything is his creation . . .

From a tiny atom to this unquantifiable cosmos , everything is his creation . . .

You don't need to believe that you have a heart, do you ?
Because you know that you are alive just because a heart is functioning with in you 24/7 hours to keep you alive.

Just like that - - -
you have to know him from with in – through your own experience
not by anyone's word

Why people who believe in GOD are being happy ?
Because they can love a being who won't leave them . . .

The universe is controlled by the creator through a set of laws . . .
Just like law of gravity and
There are many other laws which a logical mind can't decipher, except naming it .

So ' Karma ' . . .
The most popularized word in the world . . .

I don't know about other parts of the world . . .
But in India it is said that ' Your life is Your making '

I guess every one of you know this famous quote by swami Vivekananda
" YOU ARE THE CREATOR OF YOUR OWN DESTINY "

Only when you know that you are not the body and you are not even the mind , you can experience the real happiness.
Then what is that thing causing you pain. There is no doubt that our mind experiences emotional breakdown and mood swings when situations go wrong and body experiences physical pain - - - .

People suffer because they are so much identified with their body and mind. - - -

If we can create certain distance with your body , we will suffer no more and we can enjoy every moment of our life .

It is only when we relate ourselves to our body and are attached to our body so much . . . we suffer .

So , Is it possible to get to know about yourself , about the universe and about the very existence of the cosmos .

Yes , it is possible .

If you can know about you in enterity , if you can connect with the very basis of life – you can download terrabytes of data in to your system .

Having said that , You might already have the knowledge that is of a spiritual guru or enlightened person . . .

Don't believe me ?

Haven't you used the phrasing

My heart is beating so fast , My eyes are - - -

See . . .

you inherently know that our hand and heart is not us . But because of ignorance we live and die without realizing that we are not the body and we are not the mind.

If you were aware of this before, I am sure that you are already on a spiritual path knowingly or unknowingly.

So here the issue is – how to get in to spirituality and spiritual path . well we need a guru at first - without a guru it will be a path of thorns, leading to nowhere .

Everyone knows that , if we want to put an end to lifetimes of suffering we have to choose spiritual path .

So how does this works ?

Let me tell you this - If somebody smiled at the moment of death , definitely that person has little more control with the process of life .

Forget about having smile on face while dying – we are not even smiling when we are alive and healthy …

& here we are in the generation of modern technology , vaccines to lot of diseases and medication for deadly viruses , speed trains , planes , advanced computers , privilege to connect to a person who is far away from you by means of internet and lot more facilities than never before , and still we are not seeing smile on people's face …

Pain :

Let us say some person met with an accident because of a mistake that he have done while driving his car

He is going to suffer a lot of physical pain and then he is going to leave the body isn't it !

We don't have to be a sage or a guru to tell this … that at moment of death everyone is going to feel the pain …

But it is not the same with everyone

As the Karma dissipates then life energy becomes dissipates … at that time a window of opportunity will be there to leave the body with grace …

2 Enlightenment

Lotus represents enlightenment ... do you know why ?
- well that why I am here for , let's drench in the knowledge of spirituality together ...

Let's get in to the subject of enlightenment first ...

If you are living india then you might be aware of the number of possibilities to attain enlightenment . . .

- What aghori seeking and what a priest is looking are one and the same . Mukthi , Moksha , and in today's terminology 'Enlightenment'

If you are born in india you have enormous opportunity because as a civilization we are very old but as a nation we are very young and therefore there are millions of ways of experiencing realities beyond the normal way -

we know is yoga and yoga they say that it is ashtanga which means yam niyam

all of those are limbs of yogas not only you have to practice the yogasan which is physical process but also practice control over lifestyle . so that is called the right hand of god and the left hand of god is called aghora , aghora is like the sharp , short and a quick way and yoga is a long winded way but it is a safer way . There are millions of ways and an author called Robert swaboda's had written so many books about aghoras . He came to india and studied Ayurveda and as he was always attracted to aghora and the culture he came to india and found a guru and he was really attracted to our culture and then he heard all the stories about time travel and traveling to human bodies and all the supernatural powers aghora's have , so if anyone wants to choose the dark and bad way of attaining moksha then you can choose that . . . :-)

Between , I am sure no one wants to go in that way . . . hahaha ...

To rewind a little bit these are all the paths available , you can choose whichever path you want for liberation , having said that lot of spiritual gurus used to say that it is better if we don't go in to those dimensions , instead yoga is the safest way to reach the higher dimensions . There could be many ways to attain mukthi or moksha , for instance there is path called nath panth and the guru at the top of it is dath guru , these are the ways of kundalini yoga .

In Kundalini yoga , the belief is that there is a serpant coiled thrice at a base of spine and it is female energy when you practice kundalini yoga she raises through six chakras and she merges with the top chakra – and it is called that as a male and female meet , then it is said that we will have enlightenment and liberation . If you have to master kundalini yoga then you have to start from yogataravali sutras

It is said that " Jalandhara bandha , uddiyana bandha and moola bandha are situated in the throad , abdomen and perineum and by the practice of these three bandhas the dormant kundalini awakens and enters in to sushumna . The breath becomes still which is referred to as kumbhaka . with the mastery over these three bandhas the exhalation which is referred to as rechaka and the inhalation which is referred to as pooraka ceases to function and with this method the sense becomes purified and creates a path for enlightenment , they say ...

If you want to take the path of kundalini as a way to attain enlightenment then you should read the book " Moola Bandha " by swami buddhananda – I will also acquaint few more books that I have gone through to gather this knowledge , in the references page .

It is said that just Moola bandha is as effective as doing hundreds of sadhanas . The Sanskrit word moola also means root , which is firmly fixed as the source at lowest part . Everyone knows that bandha means lock and hence the name moola bandha by which it is referring to the contraction of mooladhar chakra , the seat of kundalini . Moola bandha is also known as 'perineal lock' , the contraction of the muscles around the perineal body in the male and the cervix in female in order to release and contrl energy body generated by the mooladhara chakra enables us to locate the psychic centre . It is said that once the kundalini shakti awakens and arises from sleep we rise beyond mundane realm of birth and death .

Anyway , we will discuss about kundalini in later part -

So , lets come back to our context ...

The most interesting part of our civilization is that you can encounter hundreds of paths to liberation , at liberation , one idea of liberation is something to do with rebirth the eternal cycle of rebirth and suffering and the idea of rebirth is that if you do not belive in rebirth then they say you will be free of anger , and any negative emotuions and then you will be a person having a mind with complete stability irrespective of what is happening around you . It is even said that when you are in path of yoga you can get some kind of mastery over things and that is called a siddhi .

Everyone will be having some knowledge about aghori that they basically consume human flesh and it is just one thing but there are manby . the idea there is you will go beyond idea the idea of what is good and bad , this is right and this is wrong , which is why it is called as a shortest path for detachment . Do you know that there is a simple classification in our philosy there is a classification called dev gan , manushya gan and rakshyas gan . If you belong to rakshyas gan you have a greater tendency to experience the occult practice , the person who is having dev gan can never experience occult practices an the person having manushy gan is said to have the possibility of experiencin both occult and normal ways of living . Aghora in its purest form is not abou harming human beings but it is actually a path for enlightenment .

Tantra, mantra , yantra , chakras … so and so … became Frequently used words now-a-days …

so let's discuss about them first …

As acquainted in the other half of the book chakras are nothing but energy centres …

3 Chakras and Kundalini Yoga

Chakras :

Chakras are the central energy points with in the points.

It is said that Chakras are interconnected to the 5 elements being Earth, Water , Fire , Air and Ether which in English terms called as space .

The meaning of chakras can never be fully explained in words , they must be experienced to be understood, but at the same time , there are general attributes associated with each chakra .

There are many techniques that can be implemented to balance the chakras . one must first know what the chakras are and how they function .

A follower of my guru asked him what is 'third eye' , then

he said " *what is referred to as a third eye is not necessary an another eye like this is called as Agna chakra in yogic terminology* " .

In the pranic system there are about 72,000 Nadis these naids have 114 important junction points in the body where major meeting of connections , generally referred to as chakra …

Generally the word chakra means wheel , but these chakras that we are referring to as , are not in the form of circles or wheels , the nadis always meet in the form of triangle and the whole yogic system depends on what you do with them …

And out of these 114 important junction points in the body , 7 are held as major junction points ...

so these are the 7 chakras that everyone are talking about these days , but no one really knows them in their entirety

Mooladhara :

Also called as Root chakra

Mooladhara means foundation , this is a centre , physically located at anal outlet and genital organs ...

Mooladhara chakra marks the interface between two modes of evolution as it is the lowest chakra in man but the highest in animal.

If your energies are dominat in your mooladhara food and sleep will be the 2 major qualitites of your life and inturn they will be the most important factors in life for that person ...

By stimulating the chakra via practice of moola bandha we can raise ourselves higher , lifting our consciousness to higher dimensions .

<u>There are so many techniques and methods that you have to follow to get some mastery over this chakra ...</u>

Bhramari Pranayama – which uses breathing techniques to extend awareness,

Mooladhar Anusandhana – which focuses on feeling the presence of mooladhara chakra,

Mooladhara Dhyana – which is a guided meditation that uses visualization as a means to focus ,

Ashiwini Mudra – which focuses on muscle contraction

Vajroli Mudra – which helps to gain control over urogenital muscles , physically and mentally

Ashwini-Moola-Vajroli Mudra – which focuses on being aware of pressure points along with breathing techniques ,

Moola Bandha with Antar Kumbhaka and

Moola Bandha with Bahir Kumbhaka which uses retention as a means to get mastery over the Mooladhara chakra ...

I have mentioned clearly about each and every method in our website BODY MIND and GOD ...

So let's discuss about the next chakra , being Swadisthana ...

Swadisthana :

Also called as sacral chakra .

If your energies are dominat in your Swadisthana , which is located just above your genital organ , here you will be a pleasure seeker …

You will be someone who wants to enjoy the world

A pleasure seeker , lives little more intensely than a person who is living just for food and sleep …

So these are just different levels of intensities of energies

Manipuraka :

Also called as as navel chakra .

If you have some mastery over this chakra , helps you to manifest confidence in you

If your energies are dominat in Manipuraka , you will be doer in the world … business man , politician …

Anahata :

(Meeting between lower chakras and higher chakras)

If your energies moved to Anahata , you will be a person who wants to be creative you want to create more than simply eating , sleeping and seeking pleasure … for example an artist , they experience life more intensly

This meeting point , symbolism is two triangles meeting two upward meeting and downward meeting triangles meeting , these are two different dimensions of life – one is for self preservation and another is longing to go beyond , in your head and your heart you have longing to go beyond , but in your body you experience the longing for materialistc possesions and temporary happiness

Visuddhi :

Visuddhi means a filter in general terms .

If your energies moved in to Visuddhi , then you start functioning in a different level of competence , that people around you think you are a super human with some powers .

One dimension of visuddhi tells , that you can become occult competent . Adi yogi , shiva himself is referred to as an embodiment of Vishuddhi . If one wants to transform the situations around them , having a certain capacity of vishuddhi helps that person a lot to achieve it .

Agna :

(Referred to as wisdom center)

Among the 7 chakras , the 6th dimension is called as Agna .

Once your energy reaches Agna chakra , you will have a new clarity , a vision of life , you see everything from completely different dimension . Also called as 'Third eye' . It is said that activation of Agna chakra helps a man to see life beyond the normal limitations of perception , beyond physical .

Agna is located slightly above the area where eyebrows meet .

Sahasrara :

Also called as Thousand Petal Lotus center . Some people in spiritual path say , It will be somewhere on top of the head and some refer it as a chakra out side the physical body .

Once this chakra opens , all the layers of your karma begins to break .

Which inturn leads you towards enlightenment the ultimate bliss .

All your survival instincs are in the lower 3 chakras , self preservation is manipuraka , swadisthana and mooladhara ...

The longing to break all these barriers and go away beyong is in visuddhi , agna and sahasrara ...

It is said that if you have mastery over one chakra , it can guide you to the next one with the necessary tools ...

& mastery over these 7 chakras are possible with Kundalini yoga which brings to our next topic .

Kundalini :

It is said that kundalini arousal can take place with awkening of any one of the chakras .

However , usually it occurs with the opening of mooladhara chakra which is stimulated by moola bandha.

The word kundalini is derived from two Sanskrit words , kundela and kunda . Kundala means coiled and kunda means a pit . The kundalini is symbolized as a snake residing in a deeper place , mooladhara chakra . It is said that , it is a snake coiled around a shivalingam , the symbol of creation and represent the potential energy residing in a man . Even though the concept of kundalini is well-known in various world cultures . In english , kundalini can be translated as 'primal power' .

To Chinese people it was known as 'spiritual fire' , to African tribe 'kung' it is well known as 'n/um' and to the American Indians as 'hurakan' . In recent times , it is named as 'universal electric energy'

No matter what it is called , no matter what technique is being used , the underlying principle is essentialy the same ...

Kundalini is called as female energy and she is infact the cosmic energy in bodies and not confined to any particular physical form .

She is depicted as serpent and it is said that she sleeps in mooladhara

She sleeps because she is at rest . It is said that human's consciousness is awake to the world when she is immanent .

When she is awaken , man sleeps to the world and enjoys superworldly experience , as the union is complete within human being , he will be free from worldly pleasures .

The mind is illumintated in stages as the kundalini rises through the spinal cord , piercing the chakras . It does not travel through each chakra one by one but ascends the sushumna to the brain and sahasrara chakra where all the energy systems of chakras are wsituated . Moola bandha – the master key is for those dedicated yoga practitioners searching for the master key to unlock the abode of maha kundalini ...

Having said that , Kundalini Yoga is just one way to attain enlightenment out of all the four ways : Karma yoga , Bhakthi yoga , Raja yoga , Jnana yoga ...

Tantra mantra and yantra :

Now coming back to Tantra mantra and yantra , now-a-days lot of so called people are using those words without knowing how they work

No one really knows what is the difference between them and hence they are considering them as taboo and few people are making use of them in occult practices ...

So what exactly is Yantra !...
what is Tantra !...
what is Mantra !...

Yantra is the **tool**, tool for reaching higher possibilities ...
Tantra is the **technique** that we use to reach and
mantra is **uttering** that you do ...

Tantra does not mean unbridled practices as it is projected in horror movies. Tantra means technology , which is used to enhance the ability to manifest anything that we wished for ...

when we did not have any external tools in ancient times , we realized the need for new kind of techniques and tools that we can create using our body and to exercise this , and for this to happen

we have to explore ourselves in many different ways .

- Using our mind beyond the realm of our body is what it takes to enter in to this process called Tantra.

It is just that all kinds of wild and foolish things are practiced forgetting about the Crux of Tantra .

How effectively you do it depends on the kind of education and the intensity with which you have received the technique ...

To master any tool or technique we need a guru , a teacher , a master which brings us to the next topic ...

4 Spiritual gurus and enlightened people

Everyone knows that India is a land of seekers and Spiritual gurus were always there to guide the humanity towards enlightenment .

Lot of people might get offended by this statement , but it is not possible to attain spiritual knowledge without the help of a guru .

For me sadhguru (sadhguru jaggi vasudev) is the guiding light of my life .

I was so depressed at a point in my life , that I wanted to end it .

All because of external situations and relationships which broken me down in to pieces .

But somehow I happened to see a video of sadhguru while I was going through social media and the presence of mind that he has , the sense of humour and the grace with which he is helping people

- Simply gave me a hope , I bought his book " Inner Engineering " A Yogi's Guide to Joy , from a near by book store in bangalore and i started reading it .

So no matter , how many people put false allegations on gurus – I know the difference between the real 'Guru' and the fake 'Baba'

I guess every one can see the differences between both .

So , Let's start with my favourite guru :

Sadhguru jaggi vasudev :

Jaggi Vasudev, known publicly as Sadhguru, is an Indian yogi and author. Vasudev earned a bachelor's degree in English from the University of Mysore and has been teaching yoga in southern India since 1982 .

In 1992, he established Isha Foundation near Coimbatore, which runs a beautiful ashram and hosts a yoga centre, and has been involved in various number of activities related to spirituality, education, and the environment .

- That's what Internet says about him , if you google ... :-)

But there is much more to him ...

If you want to know about him ,

ask the people who met him already ...

Before going in detail about him ,

I thank sadhguru for creating such a beautiful place not just in the infrastructure level but the kind of atmosphere over there ... words will fall short to describe it ...

For me , the visit to isha yoga centre is an experience that I will cherish for a lifetime . Being a network engineer in bangalore I always wanted to take a break and roam around just to let go off all the work stress , but at the same time I wanted to follow my spiritual path – so I thought it would be good to visit isha yoga centre . I travelled to coimbatore alone because I wanted to experience every moment that I spent in isha yoga centre and trust me , it was and it still is the best experience that I ever had . Be it 'dhaynalinga' or the 'Adi YOGI' statue ...

Jagadish had been born on 3rd September 1957 , in mysore , a city redolent with historic and cultural associations . The vasudevs were a Telugu speaking family , based in Karnataka . Jaggi's father Dr.vasudev , a noted ophthalmologist came from an affluent family of bangalore . Being an ophthalmologist with the Indian Railways , jaggi's father had frequent transfers . As a result Jaggi changed schools several times in his childhood . Let's cut it short and get in to

the experiences he had as an adult and having said that , I have made mentioned each and every scene that happened in his childhood in our facebook page BODY MIND and GOD – If you want to know more about him , I would suggest you to go and check it out .

So , let's talk about the
turning point in sadhguru jaggi vasudev's life :

The favourite destination for most of the young mysoreans was chamundi Hill , as everyone knows that it is famous for its panoramic view and its picturesque Shakti temple of chamundeshwari . Our Jaggi , knew the hill intimately as he had been there since he was a child . It was here that he had been bitten by a venomous snake many years ago and it was down these roads that he had careened wildly on his motorcycle . It is said that one day he went up and was just sitting on a rock , He said ' *I had my eyes open and something happened , I thought it was ten minutes , but something began to happen to me . All my life I had thought , this is me , pointing to himself . suddenly I did not know which was me and which was not me . The air that I was breathing , the rock on which I was sitting , the atmosphere around me , everything had become me .*

Sadhguru Jaggi vasudev ji , even acquainted that 'the more he says about that , the crazier it will sound'

He said *"what was me had become so enormous , it was everywhere . I thought this lasted a few minutes and when I came back to my normal senses , it was about seven thirty in the evening . My eyes were open , the sun had set and it was dark . I was fully aware , but what I had considered as myself until that moment had just disappeard " .*

Interesting right ?

When I first head this story , I have shown this video of sadhguru to one of my friend explaining about the incident that happened to him on that particular day , and he thought may be sadhguru was just making up some stories , but just like sadhguru's saying "only a true seeker can see things that a logical mind can't perceive" …

Human ability to perceive is far beyond just understanding the words - But because the mind is trained right now not only to hear and record desperately , to remember and note down we are becoming like robots .

Sadhguru even tried to enlighten us in lot of events that our minds have been programmed not to see anything beyond physical to ensure the safety of our survival skills . But only a true seeker can go beyond the nature of his physical body to get to know the ultimate .

And for that YOGA is the only way ...

sadhguru always stress that there is more to human being and the ability to perceive is far more beyond what a logical mind can think ...

Ramakrishna :

Photograph of Ramakrishna, taken on 10 December 1881 at the studio of "The Bengal Photographers" in Radhabazar, Calcutta – today's Kolkata .

" Ramakrishna paramahamsa "
Ramakrishna paramahamsa :

Sri Ramakrishna Paramahansa (18 February 1836 – 16 August 1886) was an Indian Hindu mystic, saint, and religious leader in 19th century.

It is said that Sri Ramakrishna experienced spiritual ecstasies from a young age, and was influenced by several religious traditions, including devotion toward the Goddess Kali, Tantra, Bhakti and Advaita Vedanta - about which I have acquainted earlier .

As a priest at the Dakshineshwar Kali Temple, his mystical temperament and ecstasies gradually gained him widespread acknowledgement, attracting to him various spiritual teachers, social leaders, and even lay followers; he eventually taught disciples . He was generally revered by Bengali elites and within religious circles, which led to his chief disciple Swami Vivekananda founding the Ramakrishna Math, which provides spiritual training for monastics and householder devotees and the Ramakrishna Mission to provide charity, social work and education .

- Sadhguru Jaggi vasudev , a yogi , the mystic , the modern guru acquainted an incident that happened in ramakrishna paramhamsa's life - I happened to read it somewhere on internet as well , but it touched my heart when i listened to sadhguru's words in a video about ramakrishna paramahamsa .

Ramakrishna became a devotee of kaali , he took kaali as his mother he is such a devotee - his devotion knows no boundaries in such a way that his consciousness became so crystalised that if he made lunch for kaali , that form comes and eats with him , this was not imagination this is actually happening for him , because crystalised consciousness can just make it happen the way it is known to him - so actually he used to feed her and she used to eat it , food used to get empty she's danced infront of him , she ate from his own hands , what not .

She came when he called and she left him dripping with ecstasy , this may sound odd to a normal person but this was real and it was actually happening , you could have tested him chemically and unfortunately we dont have the modern technology in those times to test brains patterns .

One day he was sitting on the banks of hoogly river and a very great yogi 'thotha puri' came that way just as a guiding light for ramakrishna . Because , though ramakrishna's body mind was dripping with ecstasy whenever kaali ma comes . His inner being was longing to go beyond this ecstasy but somewhere there is a knowing that itself is a bondage , even in an extreme moment of emotion or anger there is a spot of awareness with in oneself deep down , it is just that we are empowering the emotion , sadhguru mentioned .

So coming back to ramakrishna's story , sadhguru says ramakrishna was longing somewhere but the sweetness of escstay that he is experiencing was too much to leave and go , this is not any different from a drunkard being addicted to drink . The only thing that is different is alchohol may be daming the system of drunkard and attachement towards "kaali ma" is making ramakrishna happy without any drugs but the addiction is same and the attachment is same , and the limitation is the same , but it's beautiful .

So ramakrishna whenever he had contact with 'kaali ma' , his object of devootion , he is dripping with ecstasy he don't want to leave and move on , so thota puri came and this transpired between them , thota puri said this is very simple and stated that ramakrishna has the necessary energry and he just have to empower his awarness instead of emotion and body . So ramakrishan said " ok , i will empower my awwarness and he sat in meditation but the moment he sees kali he justs flies off , then thota puri said - the next time kaali appears he have to take a sword and cut her in to pieces and then ramakrishna asks thota puri where will i get the sword from , thota puri said from the same place where you get kaali from - if you are able to create a goddess why can't you create a sword , thota puri questioned him .

Then Ramakrishna sat in meditation and the moment kali came he was dripping with ecstasy and forget to manifest the sword and the next time he sat in meditation , and this time its different - the moment ramakrishna went in to trance because 'kaali ma' came in to his consciousness , thota puri observed it and picked up a piece of glass he said , "with this peice of glass i am going to cut you - where you are struck - that i am going to cut . But when i cut that , you have to create the sword and cut the kaali down , when ramakrishna was just in edge of thota puri started cutting really deep across his forehead then ramakrishna created the sword and cut the kaali down and that's how he became free from the mother and the addiction for ecstasy that he gets by feeding of her and that's when he truly became paramahamsa , till then he is just a devotee , a child , and a lover .

Reception and legacy of Ramakrishna :

Let's take a break from Ramakrishna's spiritual life and get in to details of his legacy .

Everyone is aware of the fact that , Ramakrishna is considered an important figure in the Bengali Renaissance of 19th–20 th century. So many organisations have been established in his name . But , the Ramakrishna Math and Mission is the main organisation founded by Swami Vivekananda in 1897 , I guess there is no need to introduce who swami Vivekananda is . . .

The Mission conducts extensive work in health care, disaster relief, rural management, tribal welfare, elementary and higher education and what not , the Mission conducts everything from A to Z . . .

The movement is considered as one of the revitalisation movements of India.

Amiya Sen , known an author for so many books , writes that Vivekananda's "social service gospel" stemmed from direct inspiration from Ramakrishna and rests significantly on the "liminal quality" of his Master Ramakrishna paramahamsa's message.

It is not only Swami Vivekananda , there are so many people who established organisations and helped in charity . . . organisations such as the Ramakrishna Vedanta Society founded which was founded by Swami Abhedananda in 1923, the Ramakrishna Sarada Math founded by a rebel group in 1929, the Sri Sarada Math and Ramakrishna Sarada Mission founded in 1959 as a sister organisation by the Ramakrishna Math and Mission and the Ramakrishna Vivekananda Mission formed by Swami Nityananda in 1976 .

Rabindranath Tagore about Ramakrishna :

Just like the saying , great minds are alike . . .

During the 1937 Parliament of Religions, which was held at the

Ramakrishna Mission in Calcutta, Tagore acknowledged Ramakrishna as a great saint because

...the largeness of his spirit could comprehend seemingly antagonistic modes of sadhana, and because the simplicity of his soul shames for all time the pomp and pedantry of pontiffs and pundits.

Rabindranath Tagore even wrote a poem on Ramakrishna,

To the Ramakrishna Paramahamsa Deva :

Diverse courses of worship from varied springs of fulfillment have mingled in your meditation.

The manifold revelation of the joy of the Infinite has given form to a shrine of unity in your life

where from far and near arrive salutations to which I join my own.

It is not just Rabindranath tagore , so many people like him admire Ramakrishna paramahamsa as a person . . .

Mahatma Gandhi, Jawaharlal Nehru, Sri Aurobindo , Max Müller, have acknowledged Ramakrishna's contribution to humanity . . .

Birth and childhood :

As acquainted before Sri Ramakrishna ji was born on 18 February 1836, in the village of Kamarpukur, in the Hooghly district of West Bengal, India to a orthodox Brahmin family , who happened to be , a very poor, pious . Kamarpukur was untouched by the glamour of the city and contained rice fields, tall palms, royal banyans, a few lakes, and two cremation grounds. His parents were Khudiram Chattopadhyay and Chandramani Devi .

According to Ramakrishna's followers, it is said that his parents experienced paranormal and more like some supernatural incidents and visions before his birth. In Gaya his father Khudiram had a dream in which Bhagwan Gadadhara , who is a form of Vishnu, said that he would be born as his son. Chandramani Devi is said to have had a vision of light entering her womb from a near by Shiva's temple.

Everyone in the village knows that , the family was devoted to Hindu God Rama, and male children of Khudiram and Chandramani were given names that started with Ram or Rama: Ramkumar, Rameswar, and Ramakrishna . There has been some dispute about the origin of the name Ramakrishna, but there is "...evidence which proves beyond doubt that the name 'Ramakrishna' was given to him by his father..." Ramakrishna confirmed this himself, as recorded in "M"s diaries, *"I was a pet child of my father. He used to call me Ramakrishnababu."*

Ramakrishna's father died in 1843, after which family responsibilities fell on his elder brother Ramkumar.

Even though Ramakrishna attended a village school for 12 years, he later rejected the traditional schooling saying that he was not interested in a "bread-winning education".

Sounds more like me . . . :-)

But let me be frank , I am no mystic like Ramakrishna garu . . .

So coming back to the context – the village , Kamarpukur, being a transit-point in well-established means of travel , with lot of pilgrimage routes to visit for so many people , brought him into contact with holy men and renunciates .

He became well-versed in the Puranas, the Ramayana, the Mahabharata, and the Bhagavata Purana, hearing them from wandering monks .

Ramakrishna describes his first spiritual ecstasy at the age of 6

while walking along the paddy fields, a flock of white cranes flying against a backdrop of dark thunder clouds caught his vision. He reportedly became so absorbed by this scene that he lost outward consciousness and experienced indescribable joy in that state. Ramakrishna reportedly had experiences of similar nature a few other times in his childhood—while worshipping the Goddess Vishalakshi, and portraying God Shiva in a drama during the Shivaratri festival and it is said that from his 10th or 11th year of school on, the trances became common, and by the final years of his life, Ramakrishna's samadhi periods occurred almost daily. Early on, these experiences have been interpreted as epileptic seizures, and some mental health issues and these are the interpretations which were rejected by Ramakrishna himself .

As mentioned earlier , Ramakrishna's father died in 1843 . The loss of a beloved family member and his only support , drew him closer to his mother, and he spent his time in household activities and daily worship of the household deities and became more involved in contemplative activities such as reading the sacred epics. When Ramakrishna was in his teens,

the family's financial position worsened. Ramkumar started a Sanskrit school in Kolkata and also served as a priest. Ramakrishna moved to Kolkata in 1852 with Ramkumar to assist in the priestly work .

Priest at Dakshineswar Kali Temple :

In 1855 Ramkumar was appointed as the priest of Dakshineswar Kali Temple, built by Rani Rashmoni—a wealthy female jamindar of Kolkata who was well known for her kindness and benevolence to the poor and also for her religious devotion, she belonged to the kaivarta community.

Ramakrishna, along with his nephew Hriday, became assistants to Ramkumar, with Ramakrishna given the task of decorating the deity. When Ramkumar died in 1856, Ramakrishna took his place as the priest of the Kali temple .

After Ramkumar's death Ramakrishna became more contemplative. He started to look upon the image of the goddess Kali as his mother and the mother of the universe, and became desperate for a vision of her. After many days of meditation, in which he failed to receive a vision, he reportedly came to a point of such suffering that he impulsively decided to end his life , once and for all . Seeing a sword hanging in a nearby room in the temple, he ran for it and was just about to reach it and that is when , he unexpectedly had a vision of the goddess Kali for the first time . . . He became overwhelmed as he saw the Universal Mother, and before fainting, observed that to his spiritual sight, "... houses, doors, temples , the physical world and everything else vanished altogether; as if there was nothing anywhere!

And what he saw was an infinite shoreless sea of light; a sea that was consciousness. However far and in whatever direction he looked, he saw shining waves, one after another, coming towards him ."

Marriage :

Rumors spread to Kamarpukur that Ramakrishna had become unstable as a result of his spiritual practices at Dakshineswar , pity those people who spread such rumors . . .

Ramakrishna's mother and his elder brother Rameswar decided to get Ramakrishna married, thinking that marriage would be a good steadying influence upon him—by forcing him to accept responsibility and to keep his attention on normal affairs rather than his spiritual practices and visions. Ramakrishna himself mentioned that they could find the bride at the house of Ramchandra Mukherjee in Jayrambati, three miles to the north-west of Kamarpukur . The five year old bride, Saradamani Mukhopadhyaya was there in Ramchandra Mukherjee's house just like ramakrishna acquainted and they got married in 1859 . she is also considered as an avatar , later in times she was called as Sarada Devi . Ramakrishna was 23 at this point, but this age difference for marriage was typical at those times . They later spent three months together in Kamarpukur. Sarada Devi was fourteen while Ramakrishna was thirty-two. Ramakrishna became a very influential figure in Sarada's life, and she became a strong follower of his teachings. After the marriage, Sarada stayed at Jayrambati and joined Ramakrishna in Dakshineswar at the age of 18.

By the time his bride joined him, Ramakrishna had already embraced the monastic life of a sannyasi; the marriage was never effectuated. As a priest Ramakrishna performed the ritual ceremony — the Shodashi Puja in his room –where Sarada Devi was worshiped as the Divine Mother. Ramakrishna regarded Saradadevi as the Divine Mother in person, addressing her as the Holy Mother, and it was by this name that she was known to Ramakrishna's disciples. Sarada Devi outlived Ramakrishna by 34 years and played an important role in all the religious movements .

While Ramakrishna was a temple priest at Dakshineswar, wandering sadhus used to could come and stay for a while, practicing their particular mode of worship. Several of these people became Ramakrishna's teachers in some way . He had grown up practicing Bhakti to Rama. His duties as priest at the Dakshineswar temple led him to practice worship of Mother Kali.

Bhakti, Tantra, and how it helped Ramakrishna in God-realization :

It is said that , in the year 1861, he was initiated into Tantra, by Bhairavi Brahmani . Ramakrishna accepted Bhairavi Brahmani, an orange-robed, middle-aged female ascetic, as a teacher. She carried with her a stone icon representing Ram and all Vaishnava deities .

It is said that she have with her the texts of 'Gaudiya Vaishnavism' and practised Tantra. According to the her, Ramakrishna was experiencing phenomena that accompany mahabhava, the supreme attitude of loving devotion towards the divine .

The Bhairavi initiated Ramakrishna into Tantra. Tantrism focuses on the worship of shakti and the object of Tantric training is to transcend the barriers between the holy and unholy as a means of achieving liberation and to see all aspects of the natural world as manifestations of the divine shakti.

At first he began with mantra rituals such as japa and purascarana and many other rituals designed to purify the mind and establish self-control.

Under her guidance, Ramakrishna went through sixty four major tantric sadhanas which were completed in 1863. For all the sixty four sadhana, he took only a short span of three days each to complete . He later proceeded towards tantric sadhanas, which generally include a set of heterodox practices called vamachara left-hand path ,

as tantra is called a left hand of GOD , which utilise as a means of liberation, activities like eating of parched grain, fish and meat along with drinking of wine and sexual intercourse , not as a means of pleasure but as a means to break all the barriers and as a means of liberation . According to Ramakrishna and his biographers, Ramakrishna did not directly participate in the last two of those activities - some people say that he didn't indulge in meat eating nor does he practised bodily pleasures , all that he needed was a suggestion of them to produce the desired result. Ramakrishna acknowledged the left-hand tantric path, though it had "undesirable features", as one of the "valid roads to God-realization", he consistently cautioned his devotees and disciples against associating with it . The Bhairavi also taught Ramakrishna the kumari-puja, a form of ritual in which the Virgin Goddess is worshiped symbolically in the form of a young girl. Under the tutelage of the Bhairavi,

Ramakrishna also learnt Kundalini Yoga.

Hence , Bhairavi played an important part in the initial spiritual development of Ramakrishna with the yogic techniques and the tantra .

In the year 1864, Ramakrishna took up the practise of vatsalya bhava under a Vaishnava guru Jatadhari .

During this period, he worshipped a metal image of Ramlala - Rama as a child in the attitude of a mother. According to Ramakrishna, he could feel the presence of child Rama as a living God in the metal image .

Ramakrishna later engaged in the practice of madhura bhava, the attitude of the Gopis and Radha towards Krishna . During the practise of this bhava, Ramakrishna dressed himself in women's attire for several days and regarded himself as one of the Gopis of Vrindavan. According to Sri Ramakrishna, madhura bhava is one of the ways to root out the idea of sex, which is seen as an obstacle in spiritual life. According to Ramakrishna, towards the end of this sadhana, he attained savikalpa samadhi , it means he had seen god with form and qualities — he had the divine vision and he attained union with Krishna .

Totapuri and his Vedanta :

Later in the year 1865, As I said earlier in this book , a Naga Sannyasi called Thota Puri , initiated him into sannyasa and non-dual (Advaita Vedanta) meditation and transformed Ramakrishna in a way never imagined .

Totapuri first guided Ramakrishna through the rites of sannyasa—renunciation of all ties to the world. Then he instructed him in the teaching of advaita—that "Brahman alone is real, and the world is illusory; I have no separate existence; I am that Brahman alone." Under the guidance of Totapuri, Ramakrishna reportedly experienced nirvikalpa samadhi, which is considered to be the highest state in spiritual realisation. He remained in that state of non-dual existence for six months without the least awareness of even his own body.

Totapuri stayed with Ramakrishna for nearly eleven months and instructed him further in the teachings of advaita. Ramakrishna said that this period of nirvikalpa samadhi came to an end when he received a command from the Mother Kali to "remain in Bhavamukha; for the enlightenment of the people". Bhavamukha being a state of existence intermediate between samadhi and normal consciousness

In 1866, Govinda Roy, a Hindu guru who practised Sufism, initiated Ramakrishna into Islam .

and in the year 1873, Ramakrishna practiced Christianity, and had the bible read to him .

By then he got the divine knowledge from various religious paths .

After more than a decade of sadhana in various religious paths, each culminating in the realization of God by that path, his personal practices settled and he is said to have remained in bhavamukha, a level of blissful samadhi .

He would just meditate in the Temple grounds, go to the Kali temple to offer flowers to the divine Mother, and wave incense to the assorted deities and religious figures, whose pictures hung in his room.

At some point in the period between his vision of Kali and his marriage, Ramakrishna practised "dasya bhava" , during which he worshiped Rama with the attitude of Hanuman, who is considered to be the ideal devotee and servant of Rama. According to Ramakrishna, towards the end of this sadhana, he had a vision of Sita, the consort of Rama, merging into his body .

Ramakrishna's religious practice and worldview, contained all the elements of Bhakti, Tantra and Vedanta.

Ramakrishna emphasised God-realisation, stating that ,

"To realize God is the one goal in life."

Ramakrishna found that all the religions move towards the same God or divine, though using different ways , whether it is Hinduism, Christianity , Islam or any other . . .

"So many religions, so many paths to reach one and the same goal," namely to experience God or Divine.

Ramakrishna used to say , "All scriptures - the Vedas, the Puranas, the

Tantras - seek 'Him' alone and no one else."

Just like the Vedic phrase "Truth is one; only It is called by different names," .

Ramakrishna used to say that the human is always between a reality it has not yet attained and a reality to which it is no longer limited to put it in simple words , "The devotee of God wants to eat sugar, and not to become sugar."

His Style of teaching :

It is said that ramakrishna's teachings were imparted in rustic Bengali, using interesting stories . These teachings made a powerful impact on Kolkata's intellectuals .

Ramakrishna's primary biographers describe him as talkative. According to the biographers, Ramakrishna would recollect for hours about his own eventful spiritual life, tell tales, explain Vedantic doctrines with extremely mundane illustrations, raise questions and answer them himself, sing songs , crack jokes , and mimic the ways of all types of worldly people, and there by keeping the visitors captivated and enthralled all the time to pour the knowledge of spirituality in to their hearts .

Ramakrishna used rustic colloquial Bengali in most of his conversations. According to contemporary reports, Ramakrishna's linguistic style was unique, even to the people who knows the language . It contained unclear local words and idioms from village Bengali, combined with Sanskrit terms and references to the Vedas, Puranas, and Tantras. It is said that his speeches cannot be literally translated into English or any other language for that matter .

Ramakrishna was skilled with words and had an extraordinary style of preaching and educating, which have helped convey his ideas to even the most skeptical temple visitors. His speeches reportedly revealed a sense of joy and fun, but he was not at a loss when debating with intellectual philosophers . It is said that Ramakrishna's teaching style is similar to that of Socrates , I guess I don't have to explain who Socrates is . . . :-)

In a conversation with his devotee , Sri Ramakrishna said that -

It has been revealed to me that there exists an Ocean of Consciousness without limit. From It come all things of the relative plane, and in It they merge again. These waves arising from the Great Ocean merge again in the Great Ocean. I have clearly perceived all these things.

Ramakrishna regarded the Supreme Being to be both Personal and Impersonal, active and inactive:

When I think of the Supreme Being as inactive - neither creating nor preserving nor destroying - I call Him Brahman or Purusha, the Impersonal God. When I think of Him as active - creating, preserving and destroying - I call Him Sakti or Maya or Prakriti, the Personal God. But the distinction between them does not mean a difference. The Personal and Impersonal are the same thing, like milk and its whiteness, the diamond and its lustre, the snake and its wriggling motion. It is impossible to conceive of the one without the other. The Divine Mother and Brahman are one.

What is 'maya' according to Ramakrishna . . . ?

Ramakrishna regarded maya to be of two natures, avidya maya and vidya maya.

He explained that avidya maya represents dark forces of creation (e.g. sensual desire, lust , selfish actions, evil passions, greed and cruelty) which is said to keep human beings on lower planes of consciousness . These forces are responsible for human entrapment in the cycle of birth and death, and they must be fought and vanquished. Vidya maya, on the other hand, represents higher forces of creation (e.g. spiritual virtues, selfless action, enlightening qualities, kindness, purity, love, and devotion), which elevate human beings to the higher planes of consciousness . . .

Society

Ramakrishna used to teach this saying all the time

"*jatra jiv tatra Shiv* " it means wherever there is a living being, there is Shiva .

In one of his teaching, he said "Jive daya noy, Shiv gyane jiv seba" - not acting kindness to living beings , but serving the living being as Shiva Himself , is the way to live . . .

In the Kolkata scene of the mid to late nineteenth century, Ramakrishna was intolerant on the subject of 'chakri' , which is described as a type of low-paying job , a form of slavery done by few people — typically government or commerce-related clerical positions. On a basic level, Ramakrishna saw this system as a corrupted organisation that forced educated men to be servants not only to their bosses at the office but also to their wives at home. What Ramakrishna saw as the primary detriment of Chakri, however, was that it forced workers into a rigid, impersonal clock-based time structure. He saw the imposition of strict adherence to each second on the watch as a roadblock to spirituality. Regardless of this modern system , Ramakrishna demonstrated that Bhakti could be practised as an inner retreat to experience solace in the face of this Western-style discipline with discrimination in the workplace .

Swami Vivekananda described his guru Ramakrishna as an Advaita Vedantin .. .

well that brings to us , the way to start apprising the mystics of swami vivekanda . . .

Swami vivekananda

Swami Vivekananda , born as Narendranath Datta , was an Indian Hindu monk . He was a chief disciple of the 19th-century Indian mystic Ramakrishna ...

Born : 12 January 1863 , Kolkata

Died : 4th July 1902 ...

well , that's what 'google' tells about him ...

But there is much more to him than just a name , date and legacy ...

He is a great human being ...

In a video about swami Vivekananda , sadhguru jaggi vasudev ji said that , he is the first yogi who made a spiritual wave all around the western parts of the world . It is said that he went to Europe for some work and way back to united states , he happened to be a guest of a German philosopher and after dinner they met in the study table and they were discussing few things and there was aa large book on his table which is over 700 pages and the man was speaking so highly about the book , so vivekananda requested the german philosopher can you give me the book for an hour and let me see what is there in it and that man laughed and he said *"are you going to read it in one hour , I have been reading it for weeks and not getting anywhere because it is so complex and that too it is in german language you don't even know the language , what will you do"* Vivekananda said give me the book for one hour and see what is going to happen , he took the book and place between his two hands and just sast with his eyes closed after one hour he said this book doesn't have any thing of significance . . . that man thought this is the peak of arrogance , then he stated that , *"this is just arrogance , you don't even open a book and you make a comment about the book, a book which is in a language that you do not know"* . then Vivekananda challenged the german philosopher – *ask me anything about the book ,and I will tell you .*

In page 633 , what is there the german philosopher asked – verbatim Vivekananda said .

Vivekananda even acquainted him to just number the page and he will tell you what is there word by word . then the german asked how is this possib;le he said that's why they call me vivekanada . viveka means perception , his name is narendra but his guru called him viveka because of his ability to perceive .

It is said that even Nikola Tesla , the famous person in field of science gathered concepts from swami Vivekananda and Indian vedas for his world acclaimed work on Free energy .

In a speech about swami Vivekananda , Dr.A.P.J Adul kalam ji said why he admire swami Vivekananda . He mentioned , he said " My name should not be made prominent . It is my ideas that I want to be realized " …

So I want the readers of the book to remember one thing , you should admire the spiritual leaders for what they are … rather than focusing on making them popular …

Because , People on spiritual path never asks for fame rather they wish for the well being of humanity . ..

Mahavatar babaji

• You might have seen him in south Indian movie " baba " by thalaiva rajinikanth ji . Even though the movie is fitctionalized -

It is because of that movie lot of people got to know that there is a yogi who has resided for at least hundreds of years in the remote Himalayan regions ...

How I came to know about babaji :

I guess , I am in my 3rd standard ...

Those were the times , without these smart phones and high speed Internet / Wi-Fi ... children used to have lot of time to spent quality with family ...

I was always a '*baby boy*' for my grand ma ...

she used to pamper me like anything and she used to take care of all the household supplies and necessities . People used to admire her for her compassion towards people . Everything is going well and one day she revealed to us that she is not feeling well from couple of days So we got her to test ... and to our shock , she is diagnosied with cancer , Our family tried everything possible to make her well ...

As days are passing by , we wandered all across india for help , and in the process we met a disciple of Mahavatar Babaji lineage ...

He gave us a book in which lot of stories are there revealing various occurrences about Babaji ... he said few words to give us some solace from the distress that we were going through and we came back to our home ...

and somehow i opened the book and started reading it and believe me - it all happened when I was about 12 years old ...

I won't be divulging what happened thereafter , as it is going to be personal for me and my family members ...

Note : You can contact me personally , through my page BODY MIND and GOD in facebook for more info

<u>So let's get back to stories of mahavatar babaji and his milieu :</u>

• The name, MahavatarBabaji is given to him by Lahiri Mahasaya, and several of his disciples, who reported meeting him in between the year 1861 and 1935. These meetings were described by Paramahansa Yogananda himself in his book - Autobiography of a Yogi [ఒక యోగి ఆత్మకథ] . Another account was given by Sri Yukteswar Giri in his book

" The Holy Science " .

I suggest you to Read that book once , if you have the wanting to know about his work and contribuition to the humanity using spirituality as a platform ...

It is said that Mahavatar Babaji met so many people and initiated them in to spiritual path ...

• All of these accounts, along with additional reported meetings, are described in various biographies and books.

According to Yogananda's autobiography, Babaji has resided for at least hundreds and some say thousands of years in the remote regions of Himalayas, India.

• He is seen in person by only a small number of people. A report of Yogananda's own meeting with babaji is mentioned in his Autobiography .

So , I suggest you to read that book once - Irrespective of your religion, caste and creed … well , don't get angry ,

I know , I know …

we are not here just for acquainting the references …

we are here to know about him …

In recent days " Sri M " came in to limelight because of the interviews he had given to the media -

• According to his autobiography, Babaji was non other than Lord Shiva himself.

In his book, he mentions Babaji changing his form to that of Lord Shiva.

But , I would like to tell onething to you . ..

you never know what is the truth unless you start searching for it ...

• we never know what is the reality unless we start seeking for it ...

If you want to know more about Mahavatar Babaji - in detail

Go to our facebook page **BODY MIND and GOD** or write to us bodymindandgod@gmail.com for more information about spirituality and , mystics of India …

Lahari mahasaya he is the guru of sri yukteswar giri ...
• sri lahari mahasaya :
#LahiriMahasaya, was an Indian yogi and a disciple of #MahavatarBabaji.
He got the divine knowledge
of #kriyayoga from non other than Mahavatar babaji himself
Lahiri was also popularly known as Yogiraj and Kashi Baba .
• Lahiri Mahasaya was the guru of Swami Sri Yukteswar Giri - we will talk about him in later part of my upcoming posts

• Lahiri was unusual among the people, because he is the one who broke down all stereotypes.

People who know about him, used to say that he is no special than that of a conventional yogi because he lead so normal life ,in that he was a householder — married , raising a family, and doing a normal accountant job for the Military Engineering Department of the British Indian government.

• He became known in the West through Paramahansa Yogananda's autobiography . It is said that Lahiri was chosen by Mahavatar Babaji to reintroduce the lost practice of Kriya Yoga to the world

Lahiri lived with his family in Varanasi rather than in a temple or monastery.

He got a very good name among 19th century Hindu religionists.

• Even Paramahansa Yogananda's parents are his disciples - Lahiri Mahasaya foretold that the Yogananda would become a yogi.

While dutifully playing the part of a worldly man, he practised the kriya yoga and he taught the divine kriya yoga to several disciples .

• The spiritual practice which he taught to his disciples was Kriya Yoga, a series of inner pranayama practices that quickly speed up the spiritual growth of the practitioner.

It is said that Lahiri was born into a Brahmin family in a village called Ghurni [which is a neighbourhood of Krishnanagar town] in Nadia district of Bengal.

He was the youngest son of Muktakashi, wife of Gaur Mohan Lahiri. His mother left her body - when he was a child.

There is very little known about her, except that she was a devotee of Lord Shiva.

• At the age of three , he was often seen sitting in meditation, with his body buried in the sand up to his neck.

Lahiri's family ancestral home was lost in a flood, at that time he is around 5 years old , so the family moved to Varanasi, where he would spend most of his life.

As a child, he studied Urdu and Hindi, gradually moving on to Bengali, Sanskrit, Persian, French and English at the Government College.

Reciting the Vedas, bathing in the Ganges, and worship were part of his daily routine.

• Later in 1861, Lahiri was transferred to Ranikhet for his work, in the foothills of the Himalayas.

One day, while walking in the hills ...
he heard a voice calling him ...
He followed that divine voice, and then ... it lead him to none other than babaji himself ...
and the rest is history ...
Babaji helped lahiri mahasaya to regain the wisdom of his past life and Babaji taught the divine kriya yoga to lahiri mahasaya ... and he continued his daily routine just like a normal person , but while fulfilling the duties of household – as a family member who has the most responsibility for taking care of , and making decisions and creating a livelihood for the people to live in ...

- Later , a yogi , an Indian monk from his times , got the divine knowledge of kriya yoga from lahiri mahasaya himself ...
which brings to us our next person Sri yukteswar giri maharaj

to know more about mahavatar babaji , lahiri mahasaya and his disciples ... you can go to our facebook page BODY MIND and GOD ... as it is not possible to include all the details in one book , we have created series of short stories that helps you to learn about our spiritual gurus and the great people who served humanity by sharing the divine knowledge .

Sri yukteswar giri

• About Sri Yukteswar Giri (10 May 1855 – 9 March 1936) :

Sri Yukteswar Giri is the monastic name of Priya Nath Karar, an Indian monk and yogi .He is the guru of Paramahansa Yogananda

Born in Serampore, West Bengal, he was a Kriya yogi and a Vedic astrologer , a scholar of the #BhagavadGita and the Upanishads, an educator, author, and astronomer and lot more . As mentioned before - He was a disciple of Lahiri Mahasaya [acquainted in previous post]

It is said that in the late 1884 , he met Lahiri mahasaya , who became his Guru and inititated him later in to the path of Kriga Yoga . Sri yukteswar spent a great deal of time in the next several years in the company of his guru .

• He was meant for his insightful knowledge and sharp mind. He used to invite individuals from all social backgrounds to his ashrams to discuss and exchange ideas on a range of topics.

#SriYukteswargiri became a respected guru throughout Kolkata to his students who were determined to learn Kriya yoga and he also used to invit individuals regularly from all social backgrounds to his ashrams to exchange ideas and discuss on wide range of topics.

- Sri Yukteswar was considered by Yogananda as a Jnanavatar ["Incarnation of Wisdom"]

As a guru, he was nonetheless known for his candid insight, and strict disciplinary training methods, as noted by his disciple paramahamsa yogananda in his autobiography.

Sri Yukteswar giri's interest in education resulted in developing a syllabus for schools, on the subjects of physics, physiology, geography, astronomy, and astrology .

- He also wrote a book for learning basic English and Hindi called First Book, and wrote a basic book on astrology as well .

These are his words :

Look, there is no point in blindly believing that after I touch you, you will be saved, or that a chariot from heaven will be waiting for you. Because of the guru's attainment, the sanctifying touch becomes a helper in the blossoming of Knowledge, and being respectful towards having acquired this blessing, you must yourself become a sage, and proceed on the path to elevate your Soul by applying the techniques of sadhana given by the guru

- When Yukteswar giri left his body he made sure that his favourite sishya paramahamsa yogananda is not there with him.

Because yogananda won't allow him to leave his body and yet, yogananda saw his guru's divine atman [soul] ...

Don't get all teary , it is sri Yukteswar giri maharaj we are talking about . He came back again in physical form to greet paramahamsa yogananda .

I will mention about that occurrence later in this book , which brings to us ... the biography of paramahamsa yogananda . ..

Paramahamsa yogananda

If anyone asks me how is it possible to prove the power of yoga even after death then I would say there is one yogi who from our times

He is non other than Paramahamsa yogananda He was a great saint lived in our country from 1893

Just like swami Vivekananda he worked on divine plan of union of Eastren and western countries

He was a spiritual master who took the glory of India to western countries and drove them in the spiritual path

If you see his guru lineage .

You might have heard about Kriya yoga method this came outfrom this lineage .

Autobiography of a yogi is his biography it is one of the most wonderful spiritual books in the world

This book got translated in to 50 languages and it is available in all the book stores out there in market

But unfortunately no one knows the value of it

Very few who follow spiritual path , knows the value of it ...

I got addicted to it with in 2 chapters and it changed the way I see spirituality ...

• Mukunda Lal Ghosh known as sri #ParamahansaYogananda (January 5, 1893 – March 7, 1952) was an Indian monk and a yogi who transformed millions of people .

- After finishing high school yogananda formally left home and joined Mahamandal Hermitage in Varanasi ; however he soon became dissatisfied with its insistence on organizational work instead of meditation and God-Perception . He began praying for guidance and in the year 1910 , his seeking after various teachers mostly ended when he met his guru , swami sri yukteswar giri at the age of 17 .

- Everyone knows that he published his book #Autobiographyof a Yogi in 1946, since its first publishing it has sold more than four million copies ...

He introduced millions to the teachings of meditation and Kriya Yoga through his own organization #yogodaSatsangaSociety (YSS) of India, he lived his last 32 years in America.

As mentioned earlier in my previous post that paramahamsa yogananda is disciple of #sriyukteswargiri .

• He was sent by his [master] guru to spread the teachings of yoga to the West, to prove the unity between Western and Eastern religions.

He did lot of work to bring balance between Western material growth and Indian spirituality.

May be that's why he is called as "Father of Yoga in the West . It is said that yogananda was the first major Indian teacher to settle in America .

• Yogananda gained local fame there and soon he expanded his influence worldwide: went on teaching-tours, he created a monastic order, bought properties for his organization in various California locales, and initiated thousands of people into Kriya Yoga.

His book " Autobiography of a yogi " listed as one of the "100 best spiritual books of the 20th Century .

<u>His devotion towards his master sri yukteswar giri is immeasurable :</u>

He describes his first meeting with sri yukteswar as rekindling of a relationship that had lasted for many lifetimes :

" We entered a oneness of silence ; words seemed the rankest superfluities . Eloquence flowed in soundless chant from heart of master to disciple . With an antenna of irrefragable insight I sensed that my guru knew GOD , and would lead me to him . The obscuration of this life disappeared in a fragile dwan of prenatal memories . Dramatic time ! Past , present and future and its cycling scenes . This was not the first sun to find me at these holy feet ".

He would go on to train under Sri Yukteswar as his disciple for next ten years at his hermitages in Serampore and Puri. Later sri yukteswar giri informed yogananda that he had been sent to him by the great guru of their lineage , Mahavatar Babaji, for a special world purpose of Yoga dissemination and the rest is history ...

It is said that , Sri Yukteswar giri left his body in the year 1936 ...

If you want to know what happened in between those years and how yogananda became paramahamsa yogananda and how did his guru Sri Yukteswar giri left his physical body willingly – I suggest you to go our website bodymindandgod.com or you can visit our facebook page ...

As it is not possible to acquaint each and every topic in detail , I have created a platform in our facebook page to know about all spiritual gurus and their mystical occurrences ...

But , I will explain one memorable incident that happened in yogananda life that a logical mind can't dicepher ...

yogananda was sitting on his bed in a hotel in the afternoon of June 19, 1936 – suddenly he was roused from meditation by a beatific light . Before his open and astonished eyes , the whole room was transformed in to a strange world , the sunlight transmuted in to super natural splendour .

yogananda acquainted in his auto biography , " waves of rapture engulfed me as I beheld the flesh and blood form of sri yukteswar ! "

" My son ! " master spoke tenderly , on his face an angel bewitching smile .

It was For the first time in paramahamsa yogananda's life that he did not kneel at sri Yukteswar giri's feet , but instantly advanced to gather him hungrily in his arms . Moment of moments !

The anguish of past months was toll ...

" Master mine , beloved of my heart , why did you leave me ? "

Is it you ?

"Yes my child , I am the same . This is a flesh and blood body . Though I see it as ethereal , to your sight it is physical . From cosmic atoms I created an entirely new body " sri yukteswar giri maharaj replied ...

Now let's get back to the subject :

- Now-a-days , you can see lot of celebrities posting photo - holding this book " Autobiography of a yogi .

Virat Kohli ,

Steve Jobs (Former CEO of apple)

No wonder , his book is a recommended read for anyone who's interested in spirituality, Indian philosophy, especially meditation and Yoga.

<u>Time of death of paramahamsa yogananda and how did he proved his divine power :</u>

He attended a dinner in a hotel at Los Angeles ... where he preached his last spiritual speech and then he lifted his eyes to the Ajna Chakra or "spiritual eye", and while everyone is watching his body slumped to the floor and he entered mahasamadhi.

- He proved his divine power even after he died ... doctor's observed that the body didn't lose the divine traces even after the 1st 2nd and 3rd days – there were no traces of decomposition, his body didn't change colour or odor .

If anyone asks me how is it possible to prove the power of yoga even after death then I would say there is one yogi who is from our times ...

Coming to his death or let's call it as maha samadhi – here is how he proved his yogic power

On 7/Mar/1952 he attended a feast hosted by Indian ambassador at Los Angeles

Just like swami Vivekananda he too was respected by many foreigners

Towards the end , Some one asked him a question while answering him he said

A real yogi can prove the yogic power not only when life is throbbing inside of them but even after his death

The very same night sri yogananda left his body

Here is the last picture which was taken one hour before his death

Just look in to his eyes that are out of focus you can feel that they are already connected to parabrahma

observe the pure smile on his face which is beyond words

They took his body to a place called forest lawn memorial park in Los angeles .

After that surprisingly they observed that the body didn't lose the divine traces even after the 1st 2nd and 3rd days – there were no traces of decomposition .

Local doctors were astonished

Doctors kept on observing for several days . The body didn't change colour or odor .

Even though the body is not preserved and kept it out open for public to have darshan

They confirmed that it was something beyond their knowledge that they - have in science

Everyday they used to come and test and capture photos and videos

Finally doctos gave a certificate that it is far beyond their imagination ...

To know about paramahamsa yogananda garu ...

it is better if you can learn about him and his life in his own words …

The book that has changed the lives of millions ... I am sure it will change yours …

So ,

if you ask me how can "Autobiography of a Yogi" change your life !

I don't have any cut short answer , but If you want to know how … then I suggest you to Read Paramahansa Yogananda's "Autobiography of a Yogi" which is available in multiple Indian languages …

yssi.org/aoy

Translations are available in all the languages, please visit: yssi.org/aytranslations for more info …

As acquainted before Autobiography of a Yogi is one of the world's most acclaimed spiritual classics ...

As the life story of Paramahansa Yogananda — who is often referred to as the Father of Yoga in the West — this book has touched the hearts and minds of millions around the globe.

Translated into over fifty languages, it has served as an ambassador for India's ancient science of Yoga, introducing countless readers to the methods for attaining God-realization that are India's unique and lasting contribution to world civilization.

Hailed as a masterpiece from its first appearance in print in 1946, the book was honored in 1999 as one of "100 Best Spiritual Books of the Century." Today, this story of a life of unmistakable greatness continues its success in opening to the public a realm of liberating spiritual knowledge previously accessible only to a few.

Master CVV

In the year 1906 , a marriage happened between two beautiful couple , after all the rituals are completed as per the Indian tradition the priest called the bride and groom and told the groom to show arundhathi nakshtram in the sky to bride because that is a ritual usually performed by Hindus in India that after all the rituals were completed in that marriage the priest will be telling to the newly married couple to see arundhathi nakshatram and this priest did the same thing as per tradition and to her surprise she couldn't see any star in the sky , and the bride asked the priest that how can she see the star – there is not star in the sky that I can spot and say I have seen the arundhathi nakshtram , then the bride got one doubt and expressed it saying that there is no " arundhathi nakshatram " in the sky but what is the reason that everyone tells to the newly married couple to see the star – which is not visible - then the priest told to the bride that it is just a tradition for the groom to show it to the bride , but no one ever really seen it .

Then this bride happened to ask her husband , is there any thing like arundhathi nakshtram for real or it is fake . Then the groom who was silent this whole time , who had been a silent spectator during the entire conversation, listening to the priest words and looking at the situation , and considering what is happening there - touches the priest's forehead by placing his thumb finger and suddenly the priest started seeing arundhathi nakshtram and not able to handle that divine energy the priest went into a trance and fell down because of unconsciousness . After some time the priest gets back to normal state and bows down to the groom , saying that he is not a normal person and he is a divine being and he felt grateful for being the priest do to marriage for him . He is really grateful and honoured for doing his [groom's] marriage ...

Do you know who is groom in that newly married bridegroom couple , he is non other than master CVV .

Master CVV is the Aquarian Master popularly known as Master Jupiter in the Theosophical circles, who resides in the Blue Mountains. He is also known as the Master of the Nilgiri Hills. The Indians know that there is an Ashram of Agastya in the Nilgiri Mountain Range.

Before , discussing about the spiritual life and magical incidents and interesting stories about him ...

I wanted to tell you that – I happened to came across family members of Master CVV garu ... thanks to social meda ...

Recently , I have described about some of the episodes from Master CVV 's life using the knowledge that I have got through books and documentaries ...

and I happened to see a comment under my post saying " He is my great great grandfather " and the comment is from Tanvi Ramesh ...

I have contacted her and thanks to our facebook page , I have met

Jaya Chatterjee , Master CVV's granddaughter, who also happened to be grand aunt of Tanvi ...

If you want to know more about those details you can go through our page and you can contact us through bodymindandgod@gmail.com

Anyway , lets get back in to the deeper roots ... of spirituality now ...

Master CVV had a special mission to carry out for the speedier evolution of the Planetary Being and the beings of the planet as well.

Thanks to the youtube channel of Nanduri Srinivas garu , I have got some much information from the his work that he have done through his videos . So , now coming back to master CVV garu - He received from higher circles the energy connecting to Uranus, the ruler of Aquarius, which enabled him to transmit the Aquarian energies to the planet and to the beings of the planet. The use of uranium in spiritualism was not yet revealed by the Masters of Wisdom, even to the disciples of higher initiations, till 1910. Master CVV, whose mission is located in the sign Aquarius, had a spark of the metal uranium emanating from his Heart Lotus. He caused the liberation of the activity formed by it into the cosmic plane of this earth. He thereby gave stimulation to the planetary principles of his disciples. He linked up the activity of the cosmic Kundalini of the planet with that of his followers. He accomplished a double purpose by doing this. He created a possibility of quickening the spiritual evolution of man without any disturbance to the existing laws of Nature. At the same time , He also established a spiritual channel to invoke the cosmic Prana principle to aid the working of its vehicles, namely the vital body and the etheric body (body of golden light).

The Master laid out a specific plan to initiate the seekers of Truth into the Path of Immortality and cause speedier progress in relation to transmutation of the bodies and unfolding of the soul awareness.

It is said that , he gave the discipline as a triple formula:

a) Morning and evening invocation of the given sound

b) Dedicating life to service

c) To stop working for self profit.

He promised immortality to his followers; that is, transcendence of death in a cycle of 12 years, provided the related triple formula of discipline is accepted and worked out without compromise.

Master E.K., a man of steel nerves and steadfast determination and a purpose , took upon himself the discipline and worked it out with utmost sense of urgency - within the period of 12 years. He experienced death, resurrection, and thus gained the status of immortality, which is frequently called as the Third Initiation by the new groups of World Servers today.

During his years of groundwork and preparation for the ultimate - he was doing his morning prayers and rituals. He was attentively attending to the duties as a teacher , in a college . In the evenings he was giving teachings on Ramayana, Mahabharata, Bhagavad Gita and Secret Doctrine. During the later part of the 12 years groundwork, people noticed the divine charm in his face and the power in his magical work - which of his worship and teaching. He was curing people during the worship of Lakshmi-Narayana and was guiding friends through their personal problems.

Master EK

Ekkirala Krishnamacharya (Master E.K.), born on 11 August 1926 in Bapatla (India), was a university lecturer for Vedic and oriental literature at the Andhra

Master EK garu had written so many articles for several years in english and he was organizing a magazine called 'Mihira'

I have tried to gather this information about Master E.K. and the stories that are presented over here in this book are only to give a bird's eye-view of a man who lived amidst the commons, served, healed, taught, and inspired. Also keep in mind that it cannot be taken as an exhaustive account of the man who lives in the heart of many today, for no man's life can be seen in its entirety and much less can be presented. Having said that , also please be advised much remains unsaid .

The information that i have gathered about Master E.K. garu is from different websites and youtube channels .

This work is also not an attempt to deify a person, but to recollect the unusual abilities, uncommon virtues and infrequently seen practicality.

Master E.K. also had his share of mistakes, failures, and miss-conceptions just like any other human being and then only we can say a man is complete, but they are few and are far outweighed by the other noble dimensions. He was proximate to the Divine when he demonstrated noble and unusual virtues and capabilities. He was also proximate to the humans when he did mistakes. Thus, master E.K. garu stood as a good bridge for the human to cross over to the realms of Divinity and spirituality .

His strength was in his simplicity and accessibility because was not difficult to reach, he used to connect with people unlike a typical yogi / guru / baba .

He led people to understand that part of the human, which is Divine and there by enlighting people how the life works .

His life gives the message that the human being is not of the world though he is in the world. People used to get lot of doubts regarding the realm of spirituality and master E.K. used to clear lot of them .

He was not so difficult to be understood, for he was human enough.

He carried in him the scope for the future and dimensions , which needed to be reached and he carried in him the hidden dimensions of every human, which are Divine and Heavenly in nature. To put it simple – he is a mystic who's grace is available to each and every own who seeks help from him .

Thanks to tenacious and persistent demands on the people from the groups in the East and in the West - a website called world teacher posted all the information to give a brief biography of Master E.K. and I am really grateful that I found that website – most of the content that I collected about master E.K. garu is from that website .,

which I have added in the references as well .

Initial stages of master E.K garu :

Let me walk you through the - Initial stages of master E.K garu :

As acquainted before Master E.K. was born on 11th of August 1926 and to be precise it was during the evening hours on a Wednesday.

Master E.K. born in the month of Leo and so did Master CVV, Master M.N .

It has something to notify us , it seems like the universe has something to inform us , something beyond our logical mind can imagine , it is in relation to the Energy that has visited into this system through the constellation of Leo, the Energy of Synthesis.

Master E.K. was born in Bapatla, Guntur District, Andhra Pradesh, India at 5.30 p.m. I am really happy and proud to say that I am from the same state Andhra Pradesh – So I had the access and awareness about the mystics of master E.K. garu

Getting back to the crux of the content -

How master E.K. got his name :-

Everyone from Andhra Pradesh knows about Master E.K's father, Dr. E. Ananthacharya, who was a great Vedic scholar, and was also a healer of a very high order.

He took to Ayurveda and did hundreds of unbelievable and miraculous cures by using the knowledge he got in Ayurveda . No wonder why he was respected as a man of profound Vedic wisdom in those days.

When Dr. E. Ananthacharya was in deep communion and unity with the Krishna Consciousness, he conceived Master E.K. through his lady. That was the reason why the child was named after Lord Krishna as Krishnamacharya.

How master E.K's father encountered the mystics by master E.K. :-

Master E.K. was the eldest son to his father and E.K had three younger brothers. When he was 13 years of age he lost his mother. But even from childhood Master E.K. felt the guidance of his mother!

His father did not send his children to the school. He was of a very firm conviction and definite opinion that the modern schools do not teach what is to be taught. The schools make the children automated and they would mould children as per the concurrent average human thought. But that's not what Ananthacharya dreamed of - he also know that the children would lose all the thinking and creative potentials and they would settle down as ordinary amidst the multitudes if the children were sent to the modern schools . Rather , all he wanted was for his children to be much more than the average food-seeking, money-making, comfort-mongering human beings.

He thought that much time would be wasted if children were sent to school , so Dr. E. Ananthacharya, thus taught the children himself and Master E.K. learnt many intricacies of the Vedas and the inner meaning with in and its symbolism even as a child and that happened because he got the facts and the information and knowledge of spirituality from his father.

He was a brilliant child among the four and was showing a kind of brilliance right from very young age .

No doubt that Dr. E. Ananthacharya was a man of great knowledge.

He held with him the keys to the Vedas such as the the grammatical key, etymological key , the metrical key and the key of the time cycles.

His explanation of the Vedic concepts was revealing and unveiling. Gnostics, (members of the Brahma Samaj), yogis, Vedic scholars and philosophers used to meet him quite often and converse. Because he's a guide to many and every one knows he was a great source of knowledge . In spite of his busy schedule in the society, he took particular care of his four children -like mother he nursed and nourished them. Like father he initiated them into the path of knowledge and seeking for the ultimate truth .

Master E.K. garu in his childhood :

Once, when Master E.K. was of five years of age, a few members of brahma Samaj visited his father. These Gnostics discussed a lot about the Lord Absolute with Dr. E. Ananthacharya.

The Gnostics believe in the God Absolute but not the God in form. They think that to see God in a form is not the way for englightenment and they passed a declaration and stated that it is an inferior state of being to practice God as a form .

After a prolonged conversation with Dr. E. Ananthacharya, the five-year-old boy was asked to show the village in which they were living to the Gnostics. Master E.K. took them around the village and showed an important landmark in the village -a temple built for Lord Vishnu. He wished-for to the Gnostics to visit the temple. The Gnostics said: "No, we do not enter into temples". Then, he asked: "why?" The Gnostics replied cleverly : "God is everywhere, so we don't have to go and see in a temple." Then the five-year-old child asked - can't you see "If God is everywhere , is he not there in the temple ??? Why should you have any objection to get into the temple?" The

Gnostics were astonished and surprised and looked at the boy with utmost devotion and with great attention , as they didn't assume such an answer from anyone. It was like a beam of light hitting them straight on the face. They had no answer.

When they came back to home, they told Dr. E. Ananthacharya: "In your son there is some great light". Such was the stature of Master E.K. even at the age of five and that level of perception and knowledge at young age comes only for great people .

Master E.K. grew in the Vedic wisdom under the personal supervision and guidance of his father. He was a natural poet and writer. There was a grand poet of the time living in the town of Vijayawada by name Viswanath Satyanarayana. This poet was a good friend of Dr. E. Ananthacharya. One day Master E.K. wrote some poetry about the seasons of the year. and just showed it to that great poet. The poet was deeply touched by reading it because the seasons of the year were so well described and documented in an astonishing poetry. The power of Master E.K's expression, the clarity and the simplicity surprised the poet. He told Dr. E. Ananthacharya: "Your Krishna is born with a mission and a purpose . He said " I see much light in him. He seems to carry many dimensions. I admire him for what he is ". Dr. Ananthacharya .

Worship of the Mother :

Though Master E.K. had a good familiarity of the spiritual world and knowledge about vedas because of his father , he preferred the worship of the World Mother Gayatri. As he lost his mother in his early age, he was receiving a kind of motherly nourishment during the sleep hours. This lead him proximate and get close to the Mother's energy.

His father taught him the essence of the Veda. The Veda and its classifications, its complicated branches were made clear to him. The Light of the Veda is Gayatri. She is called Veda Mata, the Mother of the Veda. E.K. instinctively took to Gayatri.

To him the Gayatri mantra was the only friend and right from his seventh year he went on working with Gayatri.

By his eighteenth year he had the dream , not even dream he had the vision of mother Gayatri, the World Mother herself , in a beautiful female form and was deeply impressed by it. He relied completely upon the Mother than anything else in life. To him, the Mother Gayatri was the mother to console, a friend in need, the guide at cross-roads and the teacher to enlighten.

As he entered the university, his worship of the Mother Gayatri had touched great heights. During those days, the university was open for five days during the week, from Monday to Friday. Master E.K. used to disappear from the university hostel on Friday evenings. He was not available to the friends and colleagues and used to reappear only on Monday morning. He used to go to the Santhi Ashram, an ashram on the coastline of Visakhapatnam, and sit under a Ficus Religiosa tree from Friday evening till Monday morning. He had only one thing to do, chanting Gayatri mantra and chanting Gayatri mantra - again and again and again . . . He gained such light in his head that the students used to feel the brilliance.

He lived on water and worshipped Gayatri during the week-ends . He was a handsome man too and the brilliance in his face added dignity and gait to his facial aura. Due to the continued worship of Gayatri, his features and countenance somehow gained the female beauty. He was so attractive to look at. The men and women were equally favorable and admiring to him, and it is said that whenever he smiled - it used to ignite the spiritual life in many people . The vision in him was developed so much that he could even see the examination paper, which would come the day after in the examination hall! He could very clearly see the whole examination paper! In the beginning he was excited but he quickly shut the door on such usage of the Light. He felt it would tempt him to do many more things, causing the fall of spiritual world and he didn't want that to happen , so he clearly stopped going in the wrong direction .

When he was young, he enjoyed a few such visions, shared them discretely with his friends, but then, thanks to his discretion, he indulged not further.

He continued to meditate upon Gayatri in a means, which was really unique of him. His love for Gayatri was beyond boundaries. No wonder why he carried in him the characteristics of the Mother, he was very loveable, serviceable, patient and understanding and may be that is the reason why lot of people felt great comfort in his presence.

GRACE OF THE MOTHER :

When he was to write his post-graduation examination in literature, he was to pay money for the examination. Understaing the situation , his father sent him a money order, unfortunately which did not reach in time. He was studying in Visakhapatnam and his father was staying a little bit far - approximately 300 Km. from the place, Vijayawada. Though the money order was sent, it did not reach in time , things didn't go as planned . He was very unhappy because he could not appear for the examination. He went at once again into the shade of the Ficus Tree, and ardently worshipped the Mother. He prayed to her and said: "I cannot afford to miss this examination. I could not pay the fee in time. You are the only answer and solace to me". The Mother appeared to him and looked at him again saying: "Your fee is paid, do not worry. You will get your hall ticket". He was surprised and asked: "Who paid?" The Mother said: "It is paid". The next day, when he went to the University office, and to his surprise his name was on the list of the students who had paid the fee!

Master E.K. came out of the post-graduate examination of the University with flying colours. He stood first in the exam. That concluded his academic education. Soon he was given a job in a college at Guntur as a lecturer of Telugu. He was married to the lady Appamma, arranged by his father.

How did Master E.K knew about Master CVV :

When he set up his family in the town of Guntur, do you know what is the first thing Master E.K. did - He bought a picture of Gayatri and prepared a shrine room in the house for deeper contemplation. He had a good career and a nice job to support his family life and he thought that he should grow more into the Light of Gayatri at the same time . He decided to meditate upon the Mother Gayatri and thus he started worshipping her daily. He used to worship the Mother in the morning hours, study scriptures for an hour, have early lunch and proceed to the college. In the evening also there was the worship, followed by talks on religious and theological issues to friends and acquaintances.

Some days passed by, he was looking for the appearance of the Mother, which he had experienced two times before, but instead he started seeing something else! He started seeing a figure, a squatted figure. The figure was revealing from below upwards gradually, day after day. He was wondering: "I am planning and contemplating my vision upon the Mother Gayatri and someone else is making way into my vision". In the beginning he believed that it was an aberration, but it was not leaving him. The moment he started chanting Gayatri in the morning and evening hours, there was a little more detail of the figure appearing to him in great light. In a weekdays time, he had the total figure appearing in his vision, and that is the figure which we have as the colour picture of Master CVV garu , having said that master E.K. garu haven't met him in person nor does he knows about him.

When Master E.K. was contemplating upon the World Mother, Master CVV appeared in his vision! He did not know who he was; he had never heard of him before, not even heard his name. Master CVV was appearing when he was meditating upon Gayatri. He was surprised. Each time he contemplates in the morning, only the figure would appear to him, and smile at him. He was a bit perturbed. He was thinking: "Who is this boxer that appears to me? Where is my Mother?" (No Mother, only Master CVV). He started recollecting in his memory and thought: "Maybe it is one of those old friends of my father", but he was not getting the answer nor he is getting any solution how to find out the truth .

Everyone knows that , Master E.K. garu was known to be a very good speaker; he was a natural speaker, poet and a good teacher . He was frequently invited by lot of people to speak upon various concepts of knowledge and wisdom . One fine morning he received an invitation from a school nearby his village , where he was asked by the principal of the school to speak upon Rabindranath Tagore in the evening at seven o'clock. Master E.K. went to that village at about half past five in the evening to spend some time with the principal of the school. The principal invited Master E.K. to his house, offered him a cup of coffee, and around two minutes to six o'clock, he said: "I have a duty of fifteen minutes. Please spare me". Master E.K. asked him: "What is the duty?" The principal replied: "I have to do my prayers". Master E.K. said: "Please go ahead". As the principal entered into his prayer room, Master E.K. got the idea: "He could have invited me also for his prayers". suddenly the principal came out of the room and said: "If you don't mind, you can also join me in the prayer". So, they went in and sat in the prayer room. There, Master E.K. saw the same figure which was appearing to him recently , in the shrine, during his hours of prayer to the Mother. He was just amazed and shocked at the same time - The strange man who was appearing in his visions was just over there in the picture! The principal did the prayer, but Master E.K. was just in a different state; his joy knew no bounds, because the one whom he wanted to know was just over there. The prayer was over after fifteen minutes; then Master E.K. asked the principal: "Who is this Master? He is disturbing me quite a bit these times :-) I chant Gayatri and he appears to me daily in the morning and in the evening". Just like master E.K. the principal was equally surprised listening to what he said . To the principal only the picture of Master CVV was known, but here is a man who has seen him in his vision in the form of Light! The principal explained about Master CVV to Master E.K. - that this Master lived in Kumbhakonam, a temple town of the then composite Madras State, that he was a great Light, and that he initiated a new path of Yoga -the Yoga of Immortality, that he initiated lot of people during the 12 years period from 1910 to 1922 and that he departed in May 1922 -four years before Master E.K. was born. Then Master E.K. asked: "Would you kindly arrange a copy of his photograph for me?" The principal said yes and arranged a photograph for Master E.K. from the city of Madras. From then on Master E.K. started meditating upon Master CVV.

From the moment Master E.K. consciously came to know of Master CVV, the Master appeared and started speaking to him in the vision, saying: "You are chosen by me for a grand work and a great mission . I shall teach you from within your being. Do as I say, do as I instruct you daily in your meditation". Master E.K. agreed, and wanted to know more about the

Master. Master CVV said: "You will know as much as I reveal. As much as I inform you, you will know. From time to time you will be guided. Do as I say, if you wish to. There is no compulsion. I am pleased with you, so I have chosen you".

Bhagavad Gita, Secret Doctrine and The Divine Plan :

Master CVV started teaching Master E.K. In tune with the Plan, Master E.K. was invited by the Theosophical Society in Guntur to speak upon the symbolism of the Mahabharata. Master CVV also had his contact with the Theosophical Society when he was alive (in physical form) . So coming back to the context - Master E.K. accepted the invitation by the Theosophical Society in Guntur - After the lecture was over, Master E.K. went into the library hall of the Theosophical Society and his eyes were attracted to the book " The Secret Doctrine" written by H.P.Blavatsky, a big volume. He inquired about the book. The members of the Theosophical Society said: "It is the toughest book one can ever face. They said " We can only respect the book, we don't read it , because it is so hard to dicepher for a normal person". The day after that , Master E.K. was invited again to give one more lecture in the Theosophical Society. After that he gave many more classes to the members of the Theosophical Society on Mahabharata. When he went to the Theosophical Society on the second day, the president of the Society also came to the class, because the members had informed him that the one who was speaking on Mahabharata was speaking in such a manner that he seemed to be knowing many things. After the class, the president introduced himself to Master E.K. saying: "I am the president of the Theosophical Society and I am glad to meet you". Master E.K. replied: "There is a book titled 'Secret Doctrine' in your book shelves. Can I borrow it for a while?" The president said: "You are most welcome. No one opens that book, including me, because we don't know what is in it. We know that it is very great; more than that we don't know. Do you want to read that book? Please keep it with you" , he said . He took the book 'Secret Doctrine' home, and straight-away started reading it continuosly . There are so many new terms relating to various theologies that are used in the book and he was finding it a little bit tough to understand . It was already one o'clock in the night but he did not give up , well it is master E.K. garu that we are talking about . He just kept the book on the table and went out to have a cup of coffee in a canteen just round the corner because he was fond of coffee - having said that Master CVV, Master M.N. and Master E.K. had one common thing besides Yoga, they never refused coffee when offered; they had such a liking for coffee .

Thus, at one o'clock in the night he went to the corner of the street where there was a restaurant. He took coffee and was walking back home. Suddenly, he met a very old man on the road who asked him in English: "Would you mind offering me some food? I am hungry". The meeting was so sudden. Master E.K. looked at the man. He was a very old man, not properly dressed, with a pen in his shirt pocket. The marks of ink were all over the pocket. He had grey long hair and a barb. The old man asked him for the second time in English: "Would you mind offering me something? I am hungry". Master E.K. said: "Sure, please come with me, Sir". They went back once again to the restaurant, and Master E.K. asked the old man: "What would you like to eat, Sir?" He replied: " I would like to have few Chapaties". The chapaties were ordered and he was eating. Then, Master E.K. looked at the old man with greater attention. He saw that he was a very old man, very hungry, and thought: "God knows when he had eaten last! What a luck I have that I could offer something to eat to this old gentleman at this late hour of the night". He was also surprised that this old man, who was looking like a beggar, was speaking in English! Master E.K. was in a kind of thinking process while the old man was looking like he is very busy eating chapaties. Suddenly, the old man looked at Master E.K. and said: "So, you are reading Secret Doctrine". It was a shock to Master E.K. How did this old man know that he was reading Secret Doctrine? He looked at the old man with great astonishment. Then, the old man asked again: "So, you are trying to read Secret Doctrine?" Master E.K. immediately felt great veneration for the old man and said: "Yes Sir". That is all. Then, the old man said: "Get me a cup of tea". So, the topic changed. He took tea and then both of them came out of the restaurant.

On the road, as they were walking, the old man instructed Master E.K. by saying: "Before you read Secret Doctrine you read Bhagavad Gita". Master E.K., right from the childhood was reading Bhagavad Gita. He knew all the 700 slokas by heart and had given many lectures on the Gita too. So he answered the old man: "I have read Bhagavad Gita and I know all the 700 slokas by heart". The old man replied: "Before you read Secret Doctrine, read Bhagavad Gita". It was like an order. Master E.K. was surprised and thought: "Who is this man that instructs me like this? How does he know that I am reading Secret Doctrine? And with what right is he instructing me so strongly to read again Bhagavad Gita?" , because everyone knows master E.K. as the great person who know all the 700 slokas by his heart .

He was thinking so while they were walking together. He decided to read Bhagavad Gita, and wanted to convey it to the old man. He turned aside to tell him that he would do so, but when he looked aside the old man was no more and that was one more surprising incident to him that day .

Look at the irony here - Someone came, took two chapaties and tea from him, instructed him to read Bhagavad Gita and then disappeared!

So Master E.K. decided to read Bhagavad Gita again .

Master E.K. went into great focus to read The Bhagavad Gita, continuously without break till midnight of the next day. The family was not at home. He was therefore free, alone, there was no one to disturb him. While he went on reading Bhagavad Gita he had a grand vision of the Plan, which he never experienced before , he saw the Divine Plan, which is being worked out by the Inner Government, the Hierarchy of Masters of Wisdom, and the Plan of Lord Krishna for Kali Yuga. He was really thrilled.

The next day, during the midnight hours, Master E.K. went again to the same restaurant to see if he could meet the old man again. He had his cup of coffee and was loitering on the road, but to his disappointment the old man didn't show up . He started proceeding towards his house with lot of questions in his mind . Then, all of a sudden, someone from behind gently placed his hand on Master E.K's right shoulder, saying: "How is Bhagavad Gita?" He turned back and was thrilled to see the old man. He had all veneration for the old man. Immediately he touched his feet out of respect and said: "I am very grateful to you Sir, for I have found something in Bhagavad Gita". The old man replied: "Bhagavad Gita is everything; you may have found only something". Then Master E.K. asked: "Would you like to eat chapaties Sir?"

The old man said: "You should not propose anything to me. Did I propose to you yesterday, or did you propose to me? Don't propose to me. You listen to me".

Tough man - He is ! isn't he :-) .

Then he said: "Now read the book - Secret Doctrine."

In a weekdays time Master E.K. read The Secret Doctrine. When he was reading Secret Doctrine, it is said that - there were many entities coming into the house and again going out of the house. It was surprising sometimes and sometimes he even had his share of thoughts with fear : "Who are all these entities that enter into my house and go out of my house " , He gained a good understanding of the scheme of The Secret Doctrine

As he completed reading the book, the old man visited him again by walking into the house through the wall! He was not looking shabby anymore but brilliant and handsome. All that you can visualize about someone like Master K.H. and if you multiply it by one thousand times in brilliance, that was the figure Master E.K. saw. He walked through the wall and came towards him asking: "How is Secret Doctrine?" Master E.K. joined his two hands in respectful salutations saying: "Namaskarams". No more talk. Deep silence prevailed.

After a while Master E.K. asked him: "Can I ask a question Sir?" He said: "Yes". So Master E.K. asked: "How could you walk through the wall?" The Master replied: "You can also walk through". Master E.K. asked: "Can I?" Then the Master said: "Yes, in my presence you can". Then, he arranged a cot between him and Master E.K. and asked Master E.K. to walk through the cot looking at him. He said: "Just look into my eyes and walk up to me". Master E.K. did so and to his surprise , he walked through the cot up to him! . Silence prevailed again for a while in between them .

After a while Master E.K. asked again: "What for are you gracing and blessing me so much Sir?" The Grand Master said: "You are chosen for a work. The degree of purity you have and the devotion you have to the World Mother pleased many in the higher circles. I need you to work for a Plan, which I will reveal to you from time to time. It will be a very hard work for

30 years. It will not be a path of roses but a very thorny path. If you wish you can join us. The freedom is yours. But if you once accept and later deny, you will have consequences. Please remember that the Path is full of thorns. It is working for the Divine Plan, and it is not easy and simple task to do . It is like walking upon the razor's edge. You will have many crises and injuries . If you are willing, I will come back to you again". Master E.K. replied: "I am ready". Then the Grand Master said: "Don't be in a hurry. Take a weekdays time. Ponder over. You have a family, you have a vocation and you are well settled. You have the inspiration of the World Mother. Everything is comfortable in life to you and as of now everything is going well .

If only you wish, you can get in". Saying so the Grand Master disappeared. After one week he reappeared and asked: "Are you ready?" Master E.K. replied: "I am ready as I was a week ago".

Thus, the work started in 1953 with Master E.K.

He wrote more than 50+ books ranging from observations from spiritual world and commentaries on Scriptures to Homoeo- science and health . His books gave a deeper insight into Srimad Bhagavata, Astrology , Vedic hymns, Bhagavat Gita, Patanjali Yoga, Rituals, and other facets of wisdom. He also conceived four booklets for initial training of the children by the parents.

Everyone could see that the method of his writings was not at all ordinary , but it is a part of divine plan .

It was unlike the authors of the present times - whose writings were all copied from somewhere and pasted it as it is .

He used to provide inspirational and through provoking content from his own writings .

He never proposed to write anything. This was a dimension of impersonality in relation to writings.

The novels that he wrote upon the life of Lord Krishna stand out as a good example of inspirational writings it is also said that writings came through him at his will . Most of the times literatures approached him – Some people say , he never wrote; he dictated. Whenever writings approached him, he used to become suddenly very alert and ask the ones around him to pick up a pen and papers; he would start dictating and that would result in a book for the benefit of the truth-seekers. Until the subject exhausted itself, the dictation continued.

While he was giving commentaries anew on Srimad Bhagavatha, he was also diverting into other books and other areas of work. As a consequence the commentaries on Bhagavatha did not come through as expected by the groups around him. Many people had a question as to why he should not complete the commentaries on Bhagavatha and why should he get into other works of writing. When his close associates asked him for clarification he smiled and said: "People receive what is needed for the time. I am only a transmitter. I transmit immediately when it is sent to me. I do not venture to author any commentary. If it is not decided in the higher circles I prefer to wait. I do not have the habit of questioning the Ones whom I follow. As and when I receive the commentaries I would give. When it came I gave it out regardless of the time (day or night), the place (at home or on travel) and the work (while at rest or even while at work). People need to practice what is already given. Wisdom is for practice and not for information. The human mind has a mania for information, and has no inclination to practise even the fundamental steps of wisdom. To those who question for further commentaries you may emphatically tell them to practise what is already given. To you, I tell you that I am not the author. If I wanted to author books I would have given out hundreds of books arising out of my scholarly knowledge of the Scriptures, but such work would not last long. Any work conducted in tune with the Plan only survives the cycles of time."

Such impersonality was also demonstrated in his work of teaching and healing. Many of his followers are witnesses to his writings. The books Spiritual Astrology, Mandra Scripture, Music of the Soul, Man Sacrifice, commentaries on Srimad Bhagavatha, are all outstanding examples of this process of inspirational writing. When asked, he told the associates that in the Buddhic plane he gets a sudden call and his apparatus (Antahkarana Sarira) gets alerted and oriented, then he sees a script running in the ether, which he reads out for dictation, or, he sees a running movie and he describes it and this is how he dictated books. He never claimed them to be his.

Inspirational writings are not new in India. Originally, the Vedas and the Upanishads were so conceived. Scriptures such as Bhagavad Gita, Mahabharata, Bhagavata, and Ramayana, were also similarly conceived. Initiates are the fit instruments to receive wisdom from the Akashic Records to be given to the mortal beings. The decision, for the books of wisdom to manifest, happens in higher circles and through fit instruments they are transmitted. The most recent example of such transmission of wisdom has been Madam Alice A. Bailey to whom a Grand Master from Himalayas transmitted wisdom to her in New York. Today, these books of wisdom, inspire more than 3000 groups all over the planet. In the community of Initiates and disciples, clair-audience, clair-voyance, etheric movements, inspirational writings, are daily events.

Now Going back to the context ,

Master E.K. always had around him, day and night, youngsters to work for him. That helped him when he was giving dictation even during the night hours. Sometimes, the dictations were lasting for hours together. In all such cases, the youngsters were used by the turn, so that they would have adequate rest. The work went on in this manner.

The books of Master E.K., today are translated into so many languages and are doing the work of self-transformation of those who are studious in the real sense of the word. There is enough guidance in his books to set up a life of aspirant and to follow the Path of Truth. In a way, the literature he gave is complete by itself though appears incomplete for the superficial mind.

It is important to mention that Master E.K. also gave a grand poetic expression in the form of the book titled "Goda Vaibhavan", which is today considered in Telugu literature as a classical master- piece of poetry. In the circles of aspirants, this poetry is considered as unfolding volumes of spiritual practices that an aspirant can take to. It is further considered as an experience of bliss when read with devotion. The entire writings were in tune with the Plan, commenced with this book. It speaks of the spiritual practices of a fiery aspirant and her experiences of the splendour of the Truth. In a away they are the experiences of the Master himself in relation to Truth. One needs to learn

Telugu to experience the bliss that this book bestows. There is no other way, as it is impossible to bring the beauty of such poetic expression coupled with profound spiritual insights and blissful experiences.

Group Building by master E.K :

Master E.K. was often invited to various places, either for teaching wisdom or for healing through Homoeopathy. Sometimes he used to hang around for a week in a place and sometimes even a month. Wherever he went, taught and healed, groups emerged to follow the Path, which the Master was indicating, both through teaching and healing. At the end of every camp, a small group of persons urged him to guide them and also to keep the continuity of teaching and healing. The work of group building commenced in a very significant way from 1977. More than 50 groups emerged through his tours in Andhra Pradesh. Essentially, in all these groups the work of the Hierarchy has become familiar. The groups meditate, conduct healing work through Homoeo-dispensaries, and teach the wisdom either from the books of the Master or from the Scriptures or from the teachings of other Masters of India. Thus, groups emerged that work with the age-old formula of meditation, study, and service. The service activity of the groups also diversed into education and alleviation from the suffering of the poor. Service was promoted and was encouraged by him in every possible way. In all this activity of teaching, healing, and group building, Master E.K. remained impersonal. He did not specifically initiate or propose any action. To respond to the proposal but not to propose, was the chief tenet of his work.

He remained a witness to all manifestations of the work. Many a time he proclaimed: "I did not propose. I did not commence. I did not initiate". Such statements were little understood by people who have no knowledge of the qualities of Poise. He was living in the One and consequently the One Plan, of which he is a part, came into manifestation through him. It is the quality of a true Yogi "to Be but not to do". If you align your being with The Being, the work of The Being happens through the being. Such is the state of an Initiate. He allows himself to be a channel for the Divine Plan to manifest. The will individual attunes to the Will Divine. Consequently, the Will Divine functions through the individual. "Father, Thy will be done", is the Path of the disciple, the Initiate and the Master. Master E.K. was a good demonstration of this status. He never proposed. He responded to the proposals that came up to him. He never initiated any work. He was only tuning up to the work, which was already initiated in the higher circles. He was unperturbed of the results of the work and hence never sought the fruits of such work. He went on and on manifesting the work that was steered by the Guides through him.

His work concluded by the end of the calendar year 1983. Thereafter Master E.K. lived for three more months, and in March 1984 he departed. It was a 30 years work of teaching, healing, writing and moulding the lives of people in tune with the Plan. That is how the whole work started. He received instructions from time to time from this Grand Master to accomplish the work .

Preparation for the intense spiritual journey :

The period 1953 to 1965 was a period of 12 years preparation for the work to be accomplished as per the Plan conceived by those whom Master E.K. followed. There was an intensive internal training during the nights and extensive training during the days. The Masters who chose him started giving lessons relating to occultism. Copious dictations and lessons were given to him to comprehend in the field of spiritual astrology, spiritual psychology, keys to sound, colour, number and symbol. The lessons were learnt fast as Master E.K. was brilliant, attentive, and deeply devoted to what was being taught.

He was also admitted into esoteric schools of Masonry. In the period of 12 years he accomplished most advanced rituals.

The 33 volumes of the wisdom of Pythagoras were revealed to him. The chief 18 keys relating to the grand epic Mahabharata and Bhagavad Gita also got revealed. During the nights he was taught and he learnt intensely; during the day he was working intensely, as well.

He conducted daily prayers as per the direction of Master CVV, chanted the Gayatri Mantra and also performed worship to Lakshmi and Narayana (the Second Logos and His Consort). He never missed either his morning or evening prayers in spite of the esoteric work he was attending to during the nights.

During this period, Master M.N., the Pole Star relating to the Path of Immortality of Master CVV, came in touch with him. For this reason, Master E.K. was frequently visiting Ongole, where Master M.N. resided, conducted prayers and courses. He was minutely guided in all aspects of wisdom by Master M.N. also.

All this esoteric activity was conducted in utter silence and secrecy. Neither his colleagues in the college nor his friends in the society, could even have an inkling of what was happening in him. Such was the rigorous preparation. Even the family did not know a thing about the spiritual dimensions that were unfolding in him. It is interesting that it is in this period he gave birth to four sons and a daughter (later, when he was 46 years of age, he conceived the sixth child, the second daughter).

Master E.K. stands out as an example for the inner depths, outer pleasantries, strong will, deep silence and total obedience to the occult training.

CRISES:

The period of preparation was also a period of crises. The worst crisis that affected him was the ill-health of his second son which could not be cured with either the Allopathic or Ayurvedic medicinal systems. He was driven to Homoeopathy through this. With the help of a good friend who is also a Homoeopath, Master E.K. started working on his son to relieve him from the suffering of the sickness (epilepsy). Leo as he was, he carried abundant qualities of the Mother, besides, he was also an ardent follower of the World Mother. To him suffering of any being was unbearable. He was committed to alleviate suffering through this process of treating his own son. He had to make a fresh and original study of Homoeopathy to gain insight into the science. He found many dimensions which were unrecorded and consequently he could treat his son and cure him of the sickness. The crisis led him to adopt Homoeopathy as a means of healing (a therapy) for the rest of his life.

Unfortunately , During this period of 12 years he also had lot of bitter experiences – i.e., experiences of betrayal, ingratitude, criticism, which he silently bore and proceeded with the process of continuous inner unfoldment regardless the outer disturbances, disappointments and attacks. It was a period of trial and ultimate triumph. It was death to personality and birth as soul. He turned out to be a good instrument to serve humanity at large. This intense period of 12 years is generally difficult to bear with, it is equivalent of picking up ones own cross and walk the Path of Crucifixion of the personality. It is here, generally, a truth-seeker faces his tests and trials to take the real initiation into the Temple of Light.

Teaching and Healing by Master E.K garu :

Healing :

During his stay in Guntur, Master E.K was already accomplished in healing through sound, through touch, and through sight. He also got thoroughly familiar with the science of Homoeopathy. To prevent the public attraction and also the public excitement, Master E.K. chose to work through the therapy of Homoeopathy, hiding the occult powers of healing. Occult powers when demonstrated would arouse excitement in the people. This would stimulate their emotional body. When a person's emotional body is stimulated it causes not much good to the one; it causes harm, it causes imbalances in the energy system of the person. His reason gets affected, and the thinking capacities reduce to the minimum. Such an affected one would become more emotional and even fanatical to follow the personality of the teacher than The Teacher. The Teacher is the soul. The personality is the vehicle of the Teacher. Personality following, led to many religions, 'isms' and cults. It caused serious differences, and the crystallized 'isms' and religions have become a source of conflict on the planet. The Hierarchy in the New Age firmly decided to work through the main key of "impersonality". This means, no true teacher shall hereafter aggrandize himself; instead he projects the Truth, the teaching relating to it, and the path relating to it. He, as such, remains behind the activity and not before. A true teacher is expected to lead from behind, like a cowherd boy or a shepherd, but not as a warrior who leads from the front. Aquarian Age demands transparency and impersonality. The old practice of aggrandizing the personality cannot be promoted by the teacher as such. Since the major part of humanity still continues to be in the emotional plane but not in the clear mental plane, there is the personality worship to some extent relating to every teacher. However a true teacher is expected to be silent about it and, at any rate, instructed not to promote it. Master E.K., therefore, chose to do enormous healing work with Homoeopathy as a façade. His administration of Homoeopathy had many dimensions. In fact, he contributed significantly to the science of Homoeopathy by expounding certain additional qualities of the popular Homoeo medicines.

He commenced the healing work with a dispensary at home run by him and assisted by his friends. It was a free dispensary where medicine was given with love and without fee. Patients were coming and getting healed in a miraculous fashion. Slowly the word spread that he is a very special Homoeopath capable of curing incurable diseases. The dispensary grew in time and multiplied. Those who associated with him in conducting the Homoeo-dispensaries got interested to learn the science. He taught them the science and initiated them into the path of yoga of Master CVV at their instance. Those who learnt were also encouraged to operate dispensaries on their own in their localities. The Master promised visible and invisible co-operation to them, to heal the patients. As the dispensaries multiplied, he came to be known as a very generous, charitable, loving Homoeopath.

As a second and advanced step, Master E.K., encouraged even the patients who came to him to learn Homoeo and become Homoeo doctors. He is the alchemist who transformed patients into healers. He has given enormous impetus to the movement of Homoeopathy in Andhra Pradesh. Due to his inspiration, more than hundred Homoeo clinics function dispensing medicine freely to the patients today. Most of these patients, along with the medicine, were also introduced to the yoga path of Master CVV and also to the new dimensional teachings of Master E.K. The work thus unfolded chiefly through healing, while teaching and initiating work concurrently happened.

The miraculous cures done through healing are far and wide. When incurable diseases were cured, he was proclaimed as a divine person. He denied such praises and even neutralized the emotion of the people saying: “Time is the healer. When the time to get healed approaches a person, he comes to me and gets healed. The Lord of Time is accrediting me with this praise. It is not me, but it is the Lord through time. If time had not come for a person to get healed, even if he comes to me, he would not get healed. There is always a time dimension to every problem. This should not be ignored. All who do, should know this.”

He was open for healing work round the clock. He did not deny giving consultations to the sick at any part of the day. His doors for healing were kept open at all times. He always kept a telephone at his bedside to receive distant calls to give advice for cure even in sleep hours. Such was his commitment to healing. His occult power of healing came to be known in times of emergency. If a distant call came to him, he normally used to suggest a Homoeopathic remedy, but if the remedy was not immediately available he even suggested that the patient should be given placebo (sugar pills without any medicine) and used to say that it would cure. Many times it cured. Sometimes, when a patient was with him and there were no Homoeo medicines readily at hand, he used to give the patient a spoonful of water, saying that it was sacred water. It cured. At other times he cured by the word.

Once, a lady came to him in great anxiety, having been bitten by a deadly scorpion. The poison injected at the hand’s finger reached up to the shoulder. The Master smiled and touched the shoulder saying: "Did the pain reach up to this point?" The patient said anxiously: "Yes". The Master said: "It will now retrieve back. Sit for a while". Touch wood! The pain retrieved and the patient felt grateful.

Although he was demonstrating such high powers of healing, he was also conscious of the law of karma relating to the patient, as also the time dimension. He was doing his healing work dispassionately. When there were a few failures here and there, he gracefully accepted them and remained silent. Mostly he new the cause for the failure as arising out of the karma of the patient, but remained silent through the acceptance of the other's view of his failure. He never claimed infallibility. For this reason, he was dearer to those who followed him. Men who do great acts do not generally accept their mistakes and failures, but the great ones are even greater since they accept their mistakes and failures. Master E.K. was not hesitant to concede when the situation demanded; that was his greatness. His greatness was based mostly on the simplicity of goodness. Volumes can be written of the variety of healing he has done to thousands of people. He was even moulding and transforming people. He frequently used.

Homoeopathic medicine for cure, taught Ayurvedic principles to prevent the persons falling into sickness and gave the touch of the divinity for general upliftment of the patient.

TEACHING:

Teaching was the other important activity of Master E.K. Teaching and healing have been the two wings upon which he mounted meditation for transformation of those who followed him. In fact, every healer is a teacher and every teacher is a healer. They are the two inseparable functions of any true teacher. It was so in ancient days. It continues to be so with the teachers that found Truth. A teacher is inadequate if he is not a healer. Likewise, a healer is inadequate when he is not a teacher of wisdom. The ultimate purpose of the two is, to reveal the Path to the seekers who follow the teacher. Healing re-establishes the life forces to their natural equilibrium in the body, and the teaching would cause unfoldment of awareness. Unless the pranic forces are restituted to their normalcy, awareness does not unfold. Man is constituted of the life force on one side, and the force of awareness on the other side, the two being inter-twined. If one is disturbed the other is also disturbed. If one is set to order, the other also can fall into an order.

"Prana Treat, Yoga Teach" is the ancient-most concept of every teacher, and Master E.K. followed the same. He taught with patience. He taught relentlessly. He taught repeatedly. He taught with love and, when needed, he taught with power. There was humour and also hammer when he taught. He was magnetic. He was absorbing the listeners into the Buddhic state, and sometimes even into the state of Bliss. The smiles he spread while teaching were sending magnetic vibrations around and the looks were radiant to uplift the people who repeatedly looked into his eyes when he was teaching. The teaching was so attractive that people even developed listening to him as a vice. He was directly appealing to the conscience of the audience and thus was inspiring the listeners to fall into the Path of Light.

He frequently used the etymological, astrological, metrical, and cyclical keys to interpret the World Scriptures. Such usage enabled unfoldment of the hidden aspects of the scriptures such as, Ramayana, Mahabharata, Bhagavad Gita, Bhagavatha, the Old Testament and The Secret Doctrine. He was fluent in his speech either in Telugu or in English. Many a time he was critical about the orthodoxy of the religions and the crystallization of the traditions, which according to him carried fragments of Truth but not the Truth as such. He was of the strong opinion that man should approach the Scriptures afresh but not through the interpretations of the religious authorities. He was respecting the interpretations of the Scriptures by the seers, sages and saints. He was also exposing the interpolations in the Scriptures. His teachings were generally for 90 minutes; they were shorter only if the time demanded so. He never taught without a prior invocation and he never concluded the speech without the 'Peace Invocation'. He held the audience spellbound!

Another aspect relating to the Master's teaching and healing was that he never volunteered to teach or heal. Teaching and healing were done by him only when asked. If persons asked him casually, he was equally casual in his response. If people were ardent, he was equally ardent. According to the approach, his response was. He was arrogant to the arrogant, intelligent to the intelligent, escaping to the escapist, silent to the manipulative, and highly disciplining to those whom he knew as his followers.

The teaching and healing was carried out for 30 years. He not only taught the hidden side of the Scriptures but also taught to his followers the occult sciences, such as spiritual astrology, sound, colour, number, symbolism, Tantra, mantra, and even such Middle-East sciences as Ramala. He was a spontaneous teacher as and when a situation arose. He taught regardless the numbers present for the teaching in the evenings. In his work of 30 years there were hardly any days were he did not teach in the evening hours. He was frequently saying that invisibly also persons attended for their refreshment, when he taught. He also said that it was a matter of great encouragement to him when he perceived those beings. In such occasions his speech was touching very sublime states. His teachings never had a prior preparation. Each time it unfolded itself according to the need of the audience, the energy of the place, and the energy of the planetary configuration of the day. He was never seeking opinion upon his teaching. He was strictly instructed so and, hence, did not look to the opinions of the audience.

It was his style that he did not live up to the social opinion. To him, the social opinions are too shallow and temporary, and the work he needed to do was profound and therefore, many times, was not understood. Hence, his attitude to teach was one of in-forming the keen listeners (meaning, causing normalcy in the energy system of the listeners). The audience frequently expressed that many of their doubts were cleared and answered. Some expressed that they found the right guidance, others expressed that they were healed of the heaviness of their problems. The Master used to listen to them, remaining silent.

He conducted special classes during the late nights, between 9 p.m. and

12 p.m. in Homoeopathy, Astrology and other occult sciences to the young groups who were seeking intensive training in those sciences. He also taught Sanskrit with the etymological key and yoga asanas during the early morning hours.

Master E.K. broke the age-long tradition of India, which prohibited the women chanting the Vedas. The tradition also prohibited the women and the working class (the 4th class) chanting Gayatri. According to Master E.K. neither the Vedas nor Manu Dharma prohibit the women and the working class from chanting of Vedas and Gayatri. He challenged the scholars to show any authority from the Scriptures, which speak of such prohibition. He said: "The Light of Gayatri is the Light of consciousness and the wisdom of the Vedas is the wisdom of the Soul. All are souls and carry consciousness. Hence, by birth everyone is entitled to study, chant and practice Vedas and Gayatri." He also quoted this practise as existing with many seers of the past. This has offended those who follow the religious orthodoxy and they differed from his view and even denied him. Nevertheless, during the past few decades, Gayatri has become a globally popular mantra due to similar attitude, gaining momentum in India and abroad. Today, even outside India, Gayatri became popular and is been sung by hundreds of groups, if not thousands, for self-enlightenment as also for enlightenment of humanity as such. Many audiocassettes singing Gayatri Mahamantram float all around the planet.

Master E.K. was also not emphasizing upon the paraphernalia relating to Vedic rituals. He was of the view that everyone who is clean of the body and the mind, freshly dressed and who does not eat any food other than vegetarian food, is eligible to practise such rituals as Abishekam (Water Ritual), Homam (Fire Ritual) and chanting of the Vedic hymns. He was only insisting upon the correct intonation of the sounds but not upon the eligibility through caste.

He also stated that very often the statements of Krishna in the Bhagavad Gita relating to the classification of human beings into four classes, were miss-interpreted and miss-quoted. Even from Vedic times humanity was classified on the basis of their qualitative inclinations but not on the basis of birth. That class of human beings who are inclined to wisdom, to Dharmic way of living, to pursue Truth, and to live in peace, are considered as Brahmins. Another class who are inclined for martial arts, protection of others, sacrificing oneself to protect the life of a group of people, are considered as the kingly class. The third class of people are those who make intelligent utilization and exchange of natural resources for the welfare of all. They are considered as the business class. The rest of the human beings, who neither have adequate comprehension to pursue wisdom nor have the valour to protect others at the cost of their lives, or have the ability to intelligently utilize and exchange the natural resources, are categorized as the 4th class, or working class. While such divisions were done for social purposes on the basis of their quality, all are seen as human beings. The more talented ones are expected to take care of the less talented ones, and the less talented ones are expected to respect the others. It is a natural hierarchical system within the human family. The fourfold classification is not watertight and is not also determined by birth. As Krishna reiterated, the classification is clearly by quality. Master E.K. was frequently quoting this statement of Krishna and promoted the Vedic knowledge as also chanting of Gayatri to all those who are inclined to learn. He did not impose on all, regardless such inclinations. The related sloka in Bhagavad Gita is sloka 13 in book IV and goes as under:

> The I AM in all creates the social levels.
> I arrange the beings into their works according to their qualities.
> Thus I create the four classes of society.
> Know that I have done it, as the One in all of them.
> Know also that I have not done it, as the One I AM, unspendable.
> (From the book "Mandra Gita" by Master E.K. pag.234)

He always followed the essentials of Vedic conduct without compromise. He was liberal in the secondaries (non-essentials). According to him, a Vedic Aryan shall have to rise much before the Sunrise. He should offer his prayers and worship to the Lord before dawn, and complete all prayers, meditations etc., within one hour from dawn, starting as early as 4 o'clock. He admonished his associates who were late to get up and perform the morning rites. He was just loathsome to laziness. It was impossible for lazy people to be around him.

He was always clean of body and mind and was always wearing fresh clothes .

A Few incidents that showed Spiritual Dimensions of master E.K:

Master E.K. was the uncommon among the commons and yet remained common. It is uncommon to the uncommons to be common, simple and remain hidden. He is like a gem hidden by the dust, amidst many stones. It is not readily cognizable. One needs to dust himself to see the gem, which otherwise looks like any other stone. Only when situations demanded, he demonstrated the divine qualities. He never displayed them to catch the public eye, to be recognized and to be deified. His message was:

"I have come down to earth not to be worshipped by the crazy dreamers as their God once again in a new name. But I am here to be realized by the workers as their own expression of work. I AM yourself uttered forth as your own Master. Remember that you are not different from your own Master. You are in no way other than your own Master. You have no second to yourself, the 'I AM' in you. Let East and West be fused in 'ME': the 'I AM' of all. Live, work and realize ME in you."

Teachers who want to aggrandize themselves are anxious to show their spiritual powers. From the Aryan viewpoint, they are not complete, they are inadequate, they still carry a shadow of their personality. Total impersonality is the final quality of a teacher. Master E.K. did not allow himself to be known to anyone completely, nor did he make public demonstration of spiritual powers. His very close associates however knew the spiritual dimensions he carried. A few events are narrated here to give an inkling into the dimensions he carried.

****

This happened -

Once , a middle aged guy left the house without notice , , in a big family of brothers and mother . His where-abouts were not found in spite of intense search for so many days . The desperate family members approached the Master and requested for his help to locate the missing one and they wished for an answer from him . The Master winked the eyes for a split second and said: *"He is safe. He is moving southwards. He is in search of a teacher for his personal salvation. He will no more move further. I have directed him to come back. He will take to the next immediate train and come to Visakhapatnam. I have also directed him to come to me for all his salvation problems. He will reach here tomorrow afternoon and would straight away come to my house. Let him be with me for a couple of days. Later I will send him home. He will never make such escapes hereafter".*

Even though the authority with which he spoke was a wonder to the family , each and every family member knew the divine power of the master , so they kept quite and for their surprise , he returned home exactly as the Master said. He spent a couple of days with the Master and came home. The family members inquired from the fellow who left the house as to what happened to him and why he had decided to return. He said that at that moment he found in his vision Master E.K. who directed him to come back. He also said that Master E.K. volunteered to guide him in his path for salvation. The family at once became ardent followers of Master E.K.

Once the Master went along with his students in the University, to a picnic. It was a group of 30 students. Just like every other day , Master was playing with them, cracking jokes, kept the group in humour. No wonder , why the students were attracted to him . They were inspired to show their palms to Master and seek the future guidance him . The Master saw palm after palm. When he took the palm of a student he felt it cold. He looked into the eyes of the student; he was a big-eyed one; he was silent. The Master told him that the student was born to serve, serve the poorer communities. His work was to inspire the poor and the unfortunate and be their guide. He would have good name and fame. The student looked pale; he laughed away giving the impression that it would not happen. The picnic was over and the group was returning home late in the evening. The students were getting out of the bus at their respective residences. The Master did not get out of the bus until the pale one disembarked. The pale one disembarked on the road to the sea at around 10 p.m. The Master also got down the bus and took the student tenderly by the hand, looking into his eyes. Tears rolled out of the eyes of the student. He stood numb. The Master caressed the boy on the shoulders and said: "Suicide is an act of timidity. No one has ever achieved anything through suicide. Life is a great gift of God. You cannot throw away the gift to the winds. I know the agony and the conflict you suffer within. You see the unfairness of the situations and injustice of the world and the evil of selfishness . You have revolutionary ideas. You find that you are not capable of a revolution. You therefore prefer to jump into the sea tonight and terminate your life. It is not an act of wisdom, much less an act of heroism. Shun your timidity and come with me, I show you the Path". The student fell at the feet of the Master. Thereafter he received immense wisdom from the Master for 12 years. He was a source of inspiration to many in the villages.

Let me tell you one more occurrence , where Master E.K. shows his kindness and compassion to one of his close associate

This happened , one of his close associates was going to madras , now called Chennai , to inquire about the character of a man to whom a family intended to propose marriage with an young lady of the family. The associate had the habit of inform the Master whenever he went out of town. He went to the Master during the afternoon hours to take leave of him and go to Madras. The Master was in siesta. He woke up as the associate walked in and said: "Are you going to Madras?" The associate was stunned. The Master said: "Don't go. You would not be able to find anything about the man whose character you want to verify. He is a cheat. He is no doubt a Hindu Brahmin coming from a good family. He has more than one wife, a Hindu wife known in the family circles, a Muslim wife known only in the Muslim circles and has a few others. He is naive, intelligent and very mercurial. It is not easy to trace his activities. You would be a thorough failure if you go." The associate wondered and asked: "What shall I do now. I told the family that I would go to Madras this afternoon on the proposed mission. How can I tell them all this, without my knowing. Can I quote you as having said all this?" The Master said: "You may, if you think it appropriate". The associate reached the house of the family very fast and conveyed the information given by Master E.K. The family members were not happy. They said: "How can we throw away a seemingly excellent marriage alliance relying on some kind of soothe-saying?" The associate said: "To me it is truth, for I know the capacity of the Master. To me it is clear. I therefore step out of this mission. As your family friend, I suggest not to proceed further." The family respectfully disagreed. Went ahead to make inquiries about the man in Madras. They sent a retired military officer on the purpose. He made enquiries for a fortnight about the bridegroom-to-be. He came back and gave a certificate of good conduct. The marriage was performed. Three years after, all facts surfaced, to the utter dismay of the family. They came to the Master for a solution. He told the lady: "You have lost money, you have lost grace. It is now time that you get rid of that man and live alone hereafter." The affected lady came to the associate and wept saying: "It was unwise not to have followed the wise advice of a man of wisdom."

So , Every close associate of Master E.K. who believed in him used to experience the divine dimension of the master whereas the people who don't follow the suggestions of Master E.K. used to face lot of hurdles in their lives … and there are so many occasions that proved the divine knowledge that Master E.K had …

It was a treat to the mind to see how fast Master E.K. used to interpret astrological charts. Once he visited a friend's house who was the most popular and influential person in the town of Visakhapatnam. He had veneration and respect for the Master, though he was not walking the path of the Master. The friend was in excitement, for he was able to fix an excellent marriage alliance to his eldest daughter. He spoke at length about the cultural background, the social status, the economic and political powers the family of the bridegroom-to-be. The bridegroom's family had all the qualities to be regarded as noble, well known in the city of Bangalore. Master's friend was also well known due to his high positions in the national level companies. He and his family were very joyous when Master E.K. visited them. He served idlis and coffee to the Master, and explained all the details of the alliance. At the end of the conversation, suddenly, the friend asked the Master: "Master, why don't you look into the charts of the two, bride and bridegroom, and give your view." The Master said: "You have proceeded too far. There is no sense now in looking into the charts. I don't have enough freedom now to inform you on account of your committed position." The friend said: "It does not matter. I will go by what you say in spite of all that I and my family entertain in the mind. Your word is final to us. We accept it with pleasure. We know you are our well-wisher". The Master agreed to look to the horoscopes. He just looked at the horoscope of the bridegroom-to-be and in a split second he had put it off. He suddenly became serious and said: "My dear - for God's sake do not proceed with this alliance". The friend was shocked, benumbed and disappointed . Silence prevailed. After a while the friend asked: "May I know the reason for your opinion?" Master E.K. said: "Do not ask me the reason. Do not discuss further. Please close this chapter". The Master stood up and left abruptly. The friend could never realize the stand taken by the Master. It was difficult for him to accept the Master's suggestion. But he had enough respect for the Master's knowledge. In a month's time he reconciled and reluctantly put off the proposal of marriage. It was however painful to him to have lost a good alliance to his eldest daughter who was very dear to him. Six months after, one evening the friend came to the Master full of emotion and with tears in the eyes. He prostrated at the feet of the Master and said: "You are a great Master, you do not allow us to know you. You illusion us with your simplicity. You saved me from a great calamity. I now know why you have so sternly negated my daughter's marriage proposal". The Master smiled. With his two hands he held the shoulders of the friend, raised him and seated him comfortably in a chair besides him and said: "I am happy you followed the suggestion. I am bound by certain laws. I can only be suggestive to anyone. I cannot decide for others, nor can I push my view through. I suggest sincerely and wait. It is for the others to accept it or not. It depends on their karma. I knew that the boy to whom you proposed your daughter did not have long life. In fact it was very short, not even an year. Did you hear something relating to him?" The friend said, weeping: "He died in an accident". The Master consoled.

The Master's way of suggesting and directing was always subtle. If people did not follow he did not worry. He ruled himself and let others rule by themselves. He advised and guided only when asked. He was proximate and distant according to the others and was ever ready to help, only, and only when sought. It is a very refined way of functioning which is frequently unseen and unrecognized. No Master can ever be understood unless the persons around him have gained sensitivity to subtlety.

****

Once a group of intellectuals came to test Master E.K. of his knowledge and foresight. They came to the Master and exchanged pleasantries. They handed out an astrological chart and sought if the person would survive the deep sickness in which he is. They ventured to do so since they happened to be close to him in the profession. The Master took the chart, he did not even look into it and said: "Why do you waste your time and my time. I know that you have decided to waste your lives with excessive intellectualism and little effectivity. If only you had used your mental skills to benefit a few beings, your lives would have been worthy. You are demonstrating more and more unworthiness of the life given to you. I don't need to look into this chart. I can tell you that the person whom you are referring to, died a week ago. If this helps you in a way and puts you to some meaningful work hereafter, I would be happy as your colleague. The choice is always yours." The group of intellectuals felt ashamed. Of course, they did not mend their ways as they were excessively crystallized in their minds. They continue to be 'armchair critics'.

Not just in this scenario , Every person who is close to Master E.K., experienced the spiritual dimension of the Master in not just one , but so many situations ...

Once an associate of Master E.K, was travelling overnight by a train. He slept on an upper berth, which was hardly sufficient to him. He feared that he may fall during the sleep hours due to the fast movements of the train. He offered prayers to Master E.K. and slept. Around 3 o'clock in the morning, sudden brakes were applied to the train and he was about to fall. The fellow found two white brilliant hands protecting him and restoring him to the sleeping berth. He thanked the Master from the bottom of his heart. Later, when he met the Master, even before he spoke, the Master said: "You don't die if you don't sleep for a night. You could have used the night in a sitting posture contemplating upon a deity, a mantra or a Master. Don't have anxiety to sleep. Much less, plan not for sleep. Sleep comes in spite of you even if you sit. Planning for sleeping, and looking for sleeping beds, is sickness. Craving for sleep is deep sickness. Be awake and alert as far as possible." The Master and the associate smiled.

****

Many times the Master was demonstrating his knowledge of the events happening at global level. He could tell the workers around him what was happening in a remote corner of the planet. Two days after what he said used to appear in the newspapers. He used to wake up people sometimes during the midnight hours and ask them to join him in meditation. The meditation used to be of 2 to 3 hours duration, in utter silence. The next day morning when inquired, he told his workers: "Certain great beings are descending on to the planet via the moon-rays. They are Venusian beings. They come to assist the Divine Plan and help lifting up this humanity. The Hierarchy is receiving them with utmost veneration. I chose to wake you up for I do not want you to sleep during such sublime times".

****

Once, he was sitting in a relaxed manner in a chair, looking to a roof corner of the room. Suddenly a laughter broke out of him. An associate who was there, asked him the reason for the laughter. The Master said: "It is delicate and too sensitive. Nevertheless I share it with you. The fellow whom I sent to Belgium is drinking whiskey. It is too cold over there. His comrades suggested whisky to warm up. Poor fellow, he is afraid of me that I may know. He took two sips of whisky and put it off out of fear of me. I would have been happier had he taken the whole glass. The laughter is for that reason". The associate asked: "Do you often see things like this?" The Master said: "No I do not. It is not my business at all. I do not enter into the private chambers of anyone's mind. I enter when invited and not otherwise. Our fellow in Belgium thought of me while drinking whisky, hence my attention was drawn to him. That is all there is to it".

Every close associate of Master E.K. experienced the spiritual dimension of the Master in one or more facets of his life. That built the cordiality for deeper association with the Master.

The Teachings of the Master :

The teachings of Master E.K. have been simple, straight and are capable to adaptation to daily life. Wisdom applicable to daily living is the live wisdom. He was demonstrating such wisdom in life, while he was capable of the most abstract ideation. Practicality has been the key-note of his functioning. Expression of wisdom through work has been his strength. Communication of the sublime Truth through simple sentences of conversation has been his speciality. He was a teacher in the true spirit of the word. He could teach an infant and a philosopher at the same time. He could inspire an uneducated, simple, housewife to the most educated and sophisticated persons. The strength of his wisdom was in his equanimity. To him God exists everywhere, at all times, in all places, in all forms and in all names. Observing him was a delight. Seldom he stepped out of the Soul Consciousness. In spite of such atunement, he was humorous enough. It does not mean that he always laughed and joked. He was fiery, angry, jovial, quiet, active, deeply silent, as per the situations.

In my view the teacher as such, stands heads and shoulders above all that he teaches. He is the presentation of Truth. Teaching is a fragment of it. Once, when he was asked to give the teachings of the World Teacher, he said: "The Presence of the World Teacher is the sum and essence of all teachings. His teachings do not stand comparison to his Presence. Learn to experience such Presence, while you may occasionally engage with the teachings. Orientation to teaching is generally mental. Such orientation should lead to experiencing of the Presence. The Presence is the ultimate of all teachings."

For aspirants who would like to follow the Path of Yoga, Truth, Light, the Master gave varied teachings through writings and utterances. The essence of all his teachings is to orient to the One Presence in all that is. The Scriptures that he mainly referred to were Bhagavad Gita, and Patanjali Yoga. He frequently used to say that Patanjali is the scientist while Krishna is the artist. Patanjali gave the science of man and the discipline that one should take to, to experience the Self. These steps of discipline, put together, are called Discipleship. Krishna presents the steps in an artistic manner in Bhagavad Gita. The yoga science of Patanjali is for the practice of yoga. Bhagavad Gita goes a step ahead, to transform the practice into daily living experience.

Besides these two books, he was also frequently referring to the Bhagavatham, where disciples that reached great heights in yogic living are mentioned. The other name for world disciple is a Bhagavatha. A world disciple is one who establishes his consciousness beyond the three worlds. He lives in a state of ecstasy while he conducts his duties in the three worlds with much attention. It is the highest state where the individual muses in the Universal Consciousness and yet conducts himself effectively in all the three worlds. The other scripture that Master E.K. was referring to in his writings and teachings, and even in advanced rituals, has been Mahabharata. It was amazing the way Master E.K. revealed vistas of wisdom, applying varieties of keys to the Scripture Mahabharata.. It was his speciality.

It is said that , it was so difficult to pick and choose the gems of the teachings that came out of him. The readers would do well to pick up and read with keen interest the books that came through him. Yet the practical instructions that he gave to those who wanted to follow him, that is, follow the Path of Truth, are given hereunder.

He used to say this frequently : *"Learn to follow the Path. I do so daily. Following me is no different from following the Path. The Path exists for all. I demonstrate amidst you how to follow the Path. I have not laid any special path. The Path that exists from ancient-most times is the Path I walk and if you walk with me, you are already walking the Path. I have no other Path to lead you or guide you. I walk it; you may also walk along, if you wish. You can walk ahead if you wish; you can slow down if you wish; you can rest if you wish; you can even divert if you wish. But the Path continues to be. It is pervaded by the Great Masters of Wisdom up to the cosmic centre. It is up to you to walk or to divert. No one insists you to walk. There is no imposition. When you, as the soul, decide, you close other options by yourself and walk the Path. If you still rejoice in other options, the Path awaits. I have no particular glamour to lead anyone. I follow the Path and I receive from time to time guidance from the Guides. You too can do it. I have also no glamour to change this world. The world takes care of itself. What is needed is, that you take care of yourself. Wishful thinking does not change anything in you or around you in the world. Action is the key. Act, act, and act. Three times I tell you to act. While acting, learn how to act and how not to act, when to act and when not to act, where to act and where not to act. Let action be the vehicle of your progress."*

I AM, I AM THAT, THAT, THAT I AM:

The doctrine of 'I AM THAT I AM' is the ancient- most doctrine of Truth. It was Master E.K,'s most cherished topic. In Sanskrit it is presented as

AHAM ASMI, SOHAM ASMI, BRAHMA AHAM ASMI

The first step, for every aspirant, is to know that he is a column of consciousness. Other personality identities are illusion. The second step, is to know that the individual unit consciousness has no separate existence, it belongs to the Universal Consciousness. At the first step he realises I Am, at the second step he realises I Am THAT -THAT meaning the Un-definable, Universal Energy. This second step is called AHAM SAHA, I Am THAT. At the third step the individual consciousness absorbs itself into the Universal Consciousness of Existence, only THAT remains, the individual ceases to be. This state of THAT is called in Sanskrit BRAHMA AHAM ASMI. Thereafter, in the fourth step, the individual returns from THAT. He is no more the one that got absorbed into IT. He comes back as THAT only. This fourth step is called THAT I Am. This process is conceived as a mantra, which is as under:

HAMSA SIVA SO HAM

(For details please refer to the book 'Mantrams -their significance and practice' by the same composer)

These four steps are common to every truth- seeker on his way to Truth and on his return as Truth. The Hierarchy strongly emphasises the fourth step of return, to serve the fellow beings, to show them the Path. Many ancient theologies speak only up to the third step of merging into THAT. The Hierarchy speaks of the return of the Initiate to serve the race. Master E.K. inevitably, in every seminar, spoke this topic which was his speciality.

So My Dear FRIENDS !

whoever is holding this book ,

I want to tell you guys onething …

We live and die without having peaceful life without experiencing what is blissfulness

Because we don't know the secret behind the true happiness

Knowing GOD = Happiness

The Rituals that we do and superstition that we have, stop us from realizing the Truth :

Right from our childhood we are made to believe in lot of stories, mythology, and tales that are built on myth.

Even our parents don't know whether the stories that they have narrated are real or not

I am not saying that all Mythologies are

Mythology creates so many rituals based on superstitions we perfom so many rituals that have no meaning and we believe in superstions that makes no sense .

Realization of the truth, Makes us undo all that has been done – a true seeker of GOD works towards that with all the energy that he have got …

It is said that liberation is possible only when one is willing to die for that – not by commiting suicide

But by

GOD is not somewhere :

Gone are the days when

Gone are the days

Gone are the days

The moment we came in to terms with reality and realize the true nature of who we are – the moment we realize that we are nothing but a mirage of the very GOD to whom we are worshipping . There won't be any other choice to us except being Blissful and happy all the time

When a man realizes that he is the soul, the life energy and a manifestation of the creator of himself he realizes that GOD is within each and every one of us

As long as we are creating attachement with every one and everything around us

We will be constantly disturbed by the sense of our body

GOD lives inside the container called as our body

GOD causes the heart to beat

There is saying that in 1000's stories lies on truth ...

We have to find on our own . . .

Having said that , lot of people will be there trying to potray myth as reality and make money out of it ...

How can we say that mythology is true when it comes from the word myth ?

we will come to that later ,

Let me tell this first ,

Do you know GODs that Japanese worship are same as that of the GOD's that Indians [Hindus] worship !!!

But now a days the divine Hindu religion is being misused because of some so called spiritual gurus ...

Having said that, still there is hope ,

hope for humanity to live in harmony

hope for spirituality to enlighten people

and hope for better tomorrow ...

As there are spiritual gurus like sadhguru , mahatria , mooji baba ...

And So is hope ...

So hope for gurus who can make us drench in ecstasy that comes from spirituality ...

rather than blindly following fake gurus and babas who are making us fools , imposing false belief systems ...

Every one in japan respect and endorse and celebrate this concept of natural superpower ...

Now coming back to the context how can we say that mythology is true when it comes from the word myth ...

Let's put it this way ... if people from two communities / religions / different grographical places , , prays same diety as the other community - probably who haven't met in person before

will that be considered as a myth ?

No right ???

well let me tell you this , recently I got to know about few deities of JAPAN ...

As I am from INDIA …
I know that , we , Hindus worship GOD GANESH
Also known as Vinayaka
Worshipped as a GOD of GOOD FORTUNE and remover of obstacles

In JAPAN, people worship GOD KANGITEN
Also known as BINAYAKA-TEN
Worshipped as a GOD of GOOD FORTUNE and remover of obstacles

In INDIA, Hindus worship LORD INDRA
Also known as King of HEAVEN and Rides on an ELEPHANT .
Worshipped as a CHIEF among DEMIGODS

In JAPAN, people worship LORD TAISHAKU-TEN
Also known as King of HEAVEN and Rides on an ELEPHANT .
Worshipped as a CHIEF among DEMIGODS

In INDIA, Hindus worship GODDESS LAKSHMI
Also known as LAKSHMI DEVI
Worshipped as the GODDESS of GOOD FORTUNE, PROSPERITY and BEAUTY .
Depicted with GOLD COINS in her hand and sitting on LOTUS FLOWER

In JAPAN, people worship KICHIJIO-TEN
Worshipped as the GODDESS of GOOD FORTUNE, PROSPERITY and BEAUTY .
Depicted with NYOIHOJU GEM in her hand and standing on LOTUS FLOWER

In INDIA, Hindus worship GOD BRAMHA
Also known as a celestial being with FOUR FACES and FOUR ARMS
Worshipped as a " Creator "
He Lords over the heavenly realm of rebirth called BRAMHALOKA

In JAPAN, people worship GOD BON-TEN
Also known as a being with FOUR FACES and FOUR ARMS
He Lords over the heavenly realm of rebirth called BRAMHALOKA

In INDIA, people worship LORD YAMA

It is said that he rides a buffalo and after death everyone has to appear before YAMA.

Also known as a CHIEF JUDGE who decides next course of action in the AFTERLIFE

In JAPAN, People worship LORD EMMA-TEN

It is said that he rides a buffalo and after death everyone has to appear before EMMA-TEN.

Also known as a CHIEF JUDGE who decides next course of action in the AFTERLIFE

CHAKRA :

In INDIA, Centres of spiritual energy in the human body is called CHAKRA

CHAKURA :

In Japanese culture,

Centres of spiritual energy in the human body is called CHAKURA

How can two completely different communities pray the same kind of dieties ... How is it possible ?

Is this all coincidence , this can't be !!! can we consider these things as myths now ???

I will give the choice to you to choose ...

There is definitely something that we can't dicepher using our logical minds ...

But , as I said before -

you never know what is the truth unless you start searching for it ... we never know what is the reality unless we start seeking for it ...

Keep following us all social media platforms : @bodymindandgod

- for more content …

Here is a list of people who shared their wisdom and made a huge wave in ocean called spirituality , I have tried to mention popular names including gurus, saints , monks, yogis and spiritual masters.

A.C. Bhaktivedanta Swami Prabhupada , Abhinavagupta , Adi Shankara , Advaita Acharya , Agastyar , Akhandanand , Akka Mahadevi ,Anandamayi Ma , Anasuya Devī , Anukulchandra Chakravarty , Arunagirinathar , Ayya Vaikundar ,Baba Hari Dass , Bahinabai , Bamakhepa Bamdev Bhairav , Basava , Bhadase Sagan Maraj , Dhanna jatt , Bhakti Charu Swami , Bhakti Tirtha swami ,

Bhaktisiddhanta Sarasvati , Bhaktivinoda Thakur , Bhaskararaya ,

Bijoy Krishna Goswami , Brahma Chaitanya, also known as Gondavalekar Maharaj , Brahmanand Swami , Brahmananda Saraswati , Chaitanya Mahaprabhu , Chandrashekarendra Saraswati

Chandrashekhara Bharati III , Charan Singh , Chattampi Swamikal

Chaturbhuj Sahay , Chinmayananda Saraswati , Chokhamela (14th century) , Dada Bhagwan - founder of Akram Vignan , Damodardev ,

Dayananda Saraswati - founder of Arya Samaj, Dnyaneshwar , Drona (mythohistorical) , Eknath (1533–1599) ,

Eknath Easwaran , Gagangiri Maharaj , Ganapati , Gaurakisora Dasa Babaji , Gnanananda Giri , Gopala Bhatta Goswami , Gopala Krishna Goswami , Gopalanand Swami , Gopi Krishna (yogi) (1903–1984) , Gora Kumbhar , Gorakhnath (c. 10th or 11th century), Gulabrao Maharaj , Gunatitanand Swami , Gurinder Singh , Gurumayi Chidvilasananda , Hans Ji Maharaj , Haridasa Thakur , Hariharananda Giri also called as Paramahamsa Hariharananda , Isaignaniyar , Jagannatha Dasa Babaji , Jiddu Krishnamurti (11 May 1895 – 17 February 1986) , Kabir (c. 15th century) Indian saint and mystic,

Mahavatar Babaji[24] (mid 18th – mid 19th century)

Mangayarkkarasiyar (c. 7th century) Tamil literature

Manik Prabhu , Master C. V. V. (4 August 1868–12 May 1922)

Mata Amritanandamayi , Matsyendranath , Meera (c. 1498 – c. 1547) Hindi literature , Mehi (28 April 1885 – 8 June 1986) , Mirra Alfassa , Morari Bapu , Mother Meera , Muktabai (c.1279 – 1297) Marathi literature , Muktanand Swami , Muktananda[15] (16 May 1908 – 2 October 1982) , Narasimha Saraswati , Narayan Maharaj , Narayana Guru, writer of Daiva Dasakam , Narayanprasaddasji Swami known as Tapomurti Shastri Swami

, Narottama Dasa (born 1466) , Narsinh Mehta Bhagat , Nayakanahatti Thipperudra Swamy (c. 15th–c. 16th century) also known as Nayakanahatti Thippeswamy , Nayanmars Saints (700–1000) ,

Nimbarka (c. 13th century) , Niranjanananda , Nirmala Srivastava, also known as Shri Mataji Nirmala Devi , Nisargadatta Maharaj , Nishkulanand Swami , Om Swami , Osho ,Panth Maharaj , Pattinathar ,

Pavhari Baba , Potuluri Virabrahmendra Swami (c. 17th century)

Prabhat Ranjan Sarkar, also known as Shrii Shrii Anandamurti , Pramukh Swami Maharaj , Pranavananda, also known as Yugacharya Srimat Swami Pranavananda Ji Maharaj , Pranavanda Saraswati ,

Prem Rawat, also known as Maharaji, Guru Maharaj Ji, and Balyogeshwar , Radhanath Swami ,Raghavendra Swami ,

Raghunatha Bhatta Goswami , Rakeshprasad , Raghuttama Tirtha ,

Ramana Maharshi[39] (30 December 1879 – 14 April 1950)

Ramanuja (c. 1017 – c. 1137)

Sai Baba of Shirdi (1838–1918)

Samarth Ramdas (1608–1681)

Sri Aurobindo (15 August 1872 – 5 December 1950)

Satchidananda Saraswati (22 December 1914 – 19 August 2002)

Sathya Sai Baba (23 November 1926 – 24 April 2011)

and many more … and it wouldn't be possible at all to mention all the spiritual leaders and gurus of India in the book …

Epilogue

Now that you have arrived at the end of this book , its time to take what you have read till now and see if you can make use of it in someway in your life .

This book was not intended to be a one time read and throw , but rather a step in process of finding your guru in life who can help in your spiritual path …

I wish you a happy , healthy and meaningful life …

Thank you once again for choosing this book …

To conclude . . . all it needs is seeking and the wanting to know

I thank each and everyone for

I am grateful for what I have been gifted with ...

will see you soon with another book ...

Till then

I hope the knowledge that you have gained by reading this book is going to help you to transform physically mentally and spiritually .

- Sri Gadiraju .

References

https://worldteachertrust.org

https://en.wikipedia.org/wiki/

Books : Autobiography of a yogi , sadhguru more than a life , Babaji and the 18 Siddha Kriya Yoga tradition , Moola bandha by swami buddhananda ,

Note : All though I have mentioned all the references that I have collected the content from in the form of bits and pieces , some people may claim for the copy rights ...

- Please be advised that the biography and history are open to everyone and the content from books and other sources that I have taken for reference are mentioned as above ...

Also be noted that , I have already taken permission to use the content from the authors and content creators ...

If you have any concerns you can contact us at bodymindandgod@gmail.com